RACHEL D FOX

Back to Me

Evolved and Unshaken - A New Awakening

**Rachel D
Fox & Co.**

First published by Rachel D Fox & Co. 2025

Copyright © 2025 by Rachel D Fox

All rights reserved. No part of this publication may be reproduced, stored or transmitted in any form or by any means, electronic, mechanical, photocopying, recording, scanning, or otherwise without written permission from the publisher. It is illegal to copy this book, post it to a website, or distribute it by any other means without permission.

Second edition

ISBN: 979-8-218-63110-9

*This book was professionally typeset on Reedsy.
Find out more at reedsy.com*

To God, my rock, my strength, my everything—none of this happens without You.
To my best friend and husband, Brent... you already know. (Seriously, no words needed. Just know.)
To my family and friends, your love, support, and occasional reality checks mean the world to me.
And to you, the reader—may these words meet you right where you are, lift you up, and remind you that your story is still being written.
With love and gratitude,
Rachel D. Fox

Contents

Dear Reader	iii
Prologue	v
The Grace in Disruption	1
Why Our Unfiltered Stories Matter Most	22
Sweet Surrender	32
When Tears Don't Follow the Script	45
Learning Life's Lessons the Long Way Around	55
Green Isn't Always Ugly	63
Fear is Not a Stop Sign	74
The Underbelly of Pride	85
Failed It, Nailed It	94
Finding Purpose in Rejection	108
Permission to Filter	124
The Quiet Roar of Courage	141
Faith Refined by Fire	151
The Woman in the Mirror	173
The Art of Truly Hearing	186
The Courage to Prioritize Your Own Well-being	202
When Pain Becomes Purpose	223
Motherhood Unfiltered	233
The Sacred Geography of Home, Heart, and Self	245
Finding Purpose in Life's Ministry	259
From My Journey Back to Yours	271
Acknowledgments	281

About the Author 282

Dear Reader

Hey there! If you've had the first version of this book in your hands, I want to start by saying a big, heartfelt *thank you*. That first edition? It poured straight out of my heart when I was right in the middle of my story. I'm not even kidding—I was writing while battling through one heck of a storm, barely seeing through the fog around me. But you know what? I don't regret putting it out there for a second. I just see now there was so much more bubbling under the surface.

This updated version? It's evolved—big time. Both in how I see things and what I'm trying to accomplish here. After tons of coffee-fueled conversations with amazing readers like you, I've realized how our personal stories aren't just ours—they're bridges connecting us to each other. This edition digs deeper, adds nuance, and honestly feels more like what I originally dreamed this book could be. My experiences are still the backbone, but now they're more like signposts on a path we're walking together, not the final destination.

For those of you coming back for round two—wow. Just wow. The fact that you're still here, still interested in this journey? That means everything to me. Your stories, feedback, and "me too!" moments have made this revised edition what it is. And if you're new here—welcome to the party! You've just stepped into a space where we laugh through tears, where strength and vulnerability hang out together, and where real change starts with looking in the mirror and sometimes saying, "Girl, what were you thinking?!"

This book has grown up into a deep dive into personal development, healing, and the beautiful thing that happens when we share our stories with each other. Between these covers, you'll find my updated take on things, plus wisdom I've collected from workshops and late-night conversations with readers from all walks of life. Each chapter is designed to show you both yourself and possibilities you might not have imagined yet.

Together, we'll figure out what it actually looks like to be authentically ourselves (messy bun days included), handle life's curveballs with something resembling grace, and build real connections by being brave enough to say, "This is me." Whether you need a shoulder to cry on, a kick in the pants, or some practical next steps, I'm hoping you find exactly what you need right now.

Can't wait to hear what resonates with you!

With so much love,
    Rachel

Prologue

Let me tell you something crazy—deciding to write this book was both the easiest and hardest thing I've ever done. Easy because I knew in my gut it was time. Hard because, hello, vulnerability hangover waiting to happen!

I can still picture the exact moment I finally committed to this whole author thing. No lightning bolt from the sky or dramatic movie moment. Just me, sitting at my messy kitchen table one random Tuesday afternoon. Kids' homework scattered everywhere, dinner prep half-started (and honestly, probably abandoned for takeout later), the beautiful chaos of real life humming all around me. And then—clarity. For example, when you've been staring at one of those Hidden Images tear-outs from Scholastic back in the '90s, suddenly, the hidden image pops out. My story needed telling, not to stroke my ego, but because it might be exactly what someone else needs to hear.

This wasn't me thinking, "Wow, my life is SO fascinating, everyone needs to hear about it!" (Trust me, my life involves plenty of unglamorous moments searching for matching socks and forgetting to make dinner). It came from all those times when I'd share a snippet of my journey with another woman, and she'd lean in close with that look—you know the one—and whisper, "Oh my gosh, I thought I was the only one." That moment of connection when someone realizes they're not alone in their struggle? Pure magic. Life-changing magic.

But can I be real with you? The doubts were LOUD. Like, screaming-in-my-ear loud. Who was I to think my experiences mattered? What made me qualified when I'm still figuring out half of this stuff myself? What if I put my heart on the page and people just... judged? These questions didn't just visit occasionally—they moved in, unpacked their bags, and started rearranging my mental furniture.

What finally shut them up wasn't suddenly feeling like I had all the answers. It was realizing something super simple but powerful: stories heal. They connect. They shine light into dark corners where we've been fumbling around alone, thinking no one else could possibly understand. If sharing mine could make even one person feel less crazy, less alone, or more hopeful—then keeping quiet wasn't an option. I didn't need to have everything figured out to offer something valuable. I just needed to tell the truth about both the mess and the magic.

The Call That Wouldn't Be Silenced

That sense of responsibility to share grew one conversation at a time. It was the young mom at my speaking event who pulled me aside with tears streaming down her face, confessing she'd been feeling like a massive failure for months but was too ashamed to tell anyone. It was my friend who, over lunch had a real honest conversation with me about anxiety and seeing a therapist. It's okay to see a therapist, y'all.

Each of these moments was like a little tap on my shoulder saying, "Hey, see what happens when you get real?" These conversations showed me something powerful: keeping my story private wasn't just a personal choice—it was potentially withholding a lifeline from someone drowning in "me too" moments. That realization flipped my thinking from "Who am I to share my story?" to "Who am I to keep it to myself?" Talk about perspective shift.

But let's not pretend there wasn't a huge granny—panty-sized gap between knowing I should write a book and actually sitting down to do it. Writing meant revisiting some chapters of my life I'd happily leave stuffed in the back of the mental closet. It meant making what had been private public and very permanent. It meant opening not just today's version of me but all my past selves—including the messy, cringe-worthy ones—to the world's judgment. (And if you think the internet isn't full of judgment, bless your heart!)

What finally pushed me to start typing wasn't some burst of courage. It was conviction. A bone-deep belief that the potential good outweighed my discomfort. I started seeing vulnerability not as weakness but as currency—the most valuable thing I could offer. If I wanted to create something truly worth your time, I couldn't serve up some sanitized, Instagram-perfect version of my life. I needed to offer something real, something honest, something with fingerprints and tear stains and highlights in different colors.

More Than Just My Story

Let's get something straight right now—this isn't just my life story bound between pretty covers. Honestly, who has time for that? This is an invitation to walk beside me, coffee in hand (wine or water bottle, or wine in a water bottle, no judgment here!), as I navigate life's wild, wonderful, sometimes ridiculous path. As you read about my adventures in love, parenthood, career reinventions, and spiritual awakenings, I hope you'll see pieces of your own story reflected back, even if the specifics look nothing like your life.

I'm not sharing all this just to document what happened to me or to process my own drama (though therapy would've been cheaper, let's be real). I'm sharing because I want to shine a flashlight on possibilities for YOUR life through the lens of mine. I want to show you that growth is messy and non-linear, that setbacks are just setups for comebacks, and that transformation often begins right when you're convinced you've hit rock bottom. I want you to see tangible proof that healing isn't just possible but inevitable when you're willing to do the work.

Instead of giving you a chronological play-by-play that would honestly bore us both to tears, I've organized this book around the big juicy themes of human experience—identity, relationships, purpose, resilience, growth. Each chapter dives into a different piece of this "finding your way back to yourself" puzzle, pulling stories from various chapters of my life to show the bigger picture. This approach lets us spot those "aha!" patterns across time, recognize how childhood stuff shapes adult decisions (fun, right?), and see how wisdom often comes from learning the same lesson fourteen different ways before it finally clicks.

Throughout these pages, I'm not just telling you what happened. I'm pulling back the curtain on what was going on in my head and heart—the thoughts, beliefs, fears, and hopes that colored everything. I'm examining the failures alongside the wins, the doubts alongside the certainties, and the questions that still keep me up at night. Because that's where the good stuff lives.

The Evolution of This Work

For those of you who read the first version of this book—thank you for coming back for round two! You might notice this edition goes deeper in ways I wasn't ready for the first time around. I've revisited, rethought, and expanded many parts of my story, opening up corners of my heart I kept safely tucked away before. This book has grown as I've grown, and I genuinely believe the new insights here are more valuable than ever.

Deciding to revise wasn't a small thing. The first edition was the absolute best I could do at that time—the most vulnerable I knew how to be, the clearest way I could share what I'd learned, the most authentic version of myself I could offer. I was proud of that work, especially when I heard from readers who found pieces of themselves in my words.

But here's the thing about growth—it doesn't stop. Life kept happening, bringing fresh perspectives and new "aha" moments. Looking back at old experiences revealed layers I completely missed the first time. Conversations with readers highlighted which parts of my story hit home hardest, suggesting where I could dig even deeper to serve you better.

The biggest surprise? Sharing my story so openly in the first edition actually accelerated my own growth. Once I'd stepped into that level of authenticity on paper, I couldn't go back to living any other way. This created this amazing cycle where being more real led to deeper insights, which then allowed me to share even more authentically. It's like compound interest, but for personal growth!

My hope is that as you flip through these pages, you'll find exactly the encouragement you need to jump into your own journey of self-discovery and growth.

A Hand to Hold on the Journey

I know exactly how it feels to think you're the only one dealing with your particular brand of struggle. I understand that special kind of loneliness that comes from believing no one else could possibly get what you're going through. I've felt that shame that whispers you should have figured things out by now, should be handling life better, should somehow be more than you are. These feelings are universal, but man, do they convince us we're uniquely messed up.

It's exactly this isolation I'm determined to disrupt by telling the unfiltered truth. When we share our real experiences—not the highlight-reel versions but the behind-the-scenes reality—we create space for others to exhale and think, "Oh thank goodness, it's not just me." We offer living proof that they're not alone, that their struggles don't define them, and that growth is not just possible but inevitable when we keep showing up.

My job isn't to hand you a step-by-step roadmap or prescribe exactly what you should do. We're all too beautifully unique for one-size-fits-all solutions. Instead, I want to show you possibilities—to demonstrate through my own messy, imperfect journey that there are multiple paths forward, that the unexpected detours often become the best parts of the story, and that you're stronger than you think you are on your worst days.

Throughout these pages, you'll find stories of love and heartbreak, hope and disappointment, massive transformation and tiny everyday miracles. You'll see the power of forgiveness (especially self-forgiveness), the necessity of self-love (not the bubble bath kind, the boundaries kind), and the life-changing impact of embracing change instead of fighting it. Through all my experiences—the good, the bad, and the "wait...what?" moments—I want to show you that no matter what obstacles are in your path right now, you have everything you need to rise above them and create a life that feels like home to your soul.

Finding Your Own Reflections

Here's where I invite you to go beyond just reading words on a page. Take a moment to really ponder the lessons and lightbulb moments I've shared, and consider how they might apply to your own unique life. Reflect on your relationships, your choices, your dreams—both the ones you've chased and the ones you've kept safely tucked away.

The real value of these stories isn't because they're so special or unique. They're valuable precisely because they're universal—because they explore those fundamental human experiences and growth processes we all go through in our own ways. While the specifics of your life will definitely look different from mine (thank goodness—can you imagine two of me in the world?!), many of the underlying patterns, challenges, and opportunities for transformation will likely make you nod and think, "I know exactly what she means!"

I encourage you not to be a passive reader here! This isn't a spectator sport. Notice which stories make you react strongly—whether with a "YES! That's exactly it!" or an "Absolutely not, I completely disagree." Pay attention when you find yourself nodding along or when something makes you uncomfortable. These reactions aren't random—they're valuable clues about your values, experiences, and areas ripe for growth.

Consider keeping a journal as you read—not just about my

story but about what it triggers in yours. What memories surface as you read certain passages? What patterns do you notice in your own life that parallel or diverge from mine? What questions pop up that might be worth exploring further? This kind of active engagement turns reading from a passive activity into a catalyst for your own insights and growth.

Remember that my journey isn't a template you need to copy (please don't—one of me is definitely enough!). The specific choices, practices, or pathways that transformed my life might not fit your unique circumstances and personality. What matters isn't that you follow my exact path but that you recognize the possibility of creating your own—one that honors both who you've been and who you're becoming.

An Invitation to Begin Your Journey Back

That phrase "back to me" means so many things, and they're all worth unpacking as we start this journey. Most obviously, it's about returning to your authentic self—rediscovering who you really are underneath all those layers of expectations, protective walls, and habits that might have disconnected you from your core. This return isn't about going backward to some previous version of yourself—it's about reconnecting with your essence while integrating everything you've learned and experienced along the way.

"Back to me" also means reclaiming ownership of your story. For too long, many of us have let others define what our experiences mean—family narratives, cultural expectations, societal judgments telling us how to interpret our own lives. Taking back this power means deciding for yourself what your experiences mean, what values matter most to you, what success looks like in your world, and how you measure growth on your own terms.

This phrase also suggests bringing attention and care back to yourself after focusing on everyone else. So many of us (especially us women) have been conditioned to put others first, to define ourselves primarily through our roles and relationships rather than our intrinsic worth. Coming "back to me" means recognizing that self-care isn't selfish but essential—that we show up more fully for the people we love when we've attended to our own well-being and growth first.

Finally, "back to me" acknowledges that this journey isn't a straight line but a spiral. We don't achieve authenticity once and forever—we find our way back to center again and again as new challenges arise, as we enter new life chapters, as our understanding of ourselves deepens. These returns aren't failures but expected parts of growth—opportunities to reintegrate at increasingly deeper levels each time.

So here we are, friend—ready to dive into this adventure together. This book is my heart in physical form. But here's what matters more—it's a mirror. As you flip through these pages of my life, my hope is you'll catch glimpses of yourself reflected back. In my stumbles and victories, my rock bottoms and mountaintops, I hope you see possibilities for your own story.

I'm so honored to walk this path with you. Together, we'll discover the power that comes from showing up authentically, the beauty that emerges from growth (even the painful kind), and the strength that's been inside you all along, just waiting to be recognized.

Welcome, friend, to the journey back to yourself. Let's do this!

The Grace in Disruption

Picture this: little me, fearlessly zooming through the neighborhood on my bike with this one crazy-steep hill that was basically our kid version of Mount Everest. I absolutely lived for that feeling—wind whipping through my hair, the rush of speed, and that perfect mix of being just a little out of control while knowing I could slam on the brakes if things got too wild.

So this one day, my friend and I got this brilliant idea to race down that monster hill. We pedaled like our lives depended on it, hearts pounding with pure excitement. But when we hit the bottom? CRASH! There we were, sprawled out on the pavement, completely winded, covered in scrapes and bruises, with little bits of gravel stuck in our skin. Talk about a reality check on just how unpredictable (and sometimes downright harsh) life can be!

That childhood bike crash is still so vivid in my memory—not just because of the physical "ouch" factor, but because of what it taught me about life's unexpected collisions. I remember that perfect moment of pure freedom flying downhill, absolutely certain nothing could possibly go wrong… followed by the sudden, jarring reality check of pavement against skin. In that split second, all my carefully laid plans (well, as "carefully laid" as a kid's racing strategy can be) completely vanished, replaced by a new, uncomfortable reality I definitely hadn't signed up for.

But here's what really sticks with me: what happened after the crash. That moment of shocked silence as my friend and I checked ourselves for damage. The slow, careful movements to figure out what still worked. The looks we exchanged that somehow contained both embarrassment and relief. And then—this is the part that gets me—the laughter. It started nervous, then turned genuine, as we helped each other up, dusted off what we could, and examined our battle wounds with this weird mix of pain and pride.

Even back then, I understood something super important about disruption: it's not just about the fall—it's about how you get back up. It's about how quickly you move from whining about your scrapes to comparing them with a certain kind of twisted delight. It's about realizing that even painful experiences can become stories you tell later with a smile, markers of resilience rather than just moments of failure.

That childhood wipeout turned out to be the perfect metaphor for all the detours and discoveries we face in life. As grown-ups, we realize our journeys are packed with ups and downs, moments of pure joy, and obstacles that come out of nowhere. Navigating these disruptions requires us to be resilient, adaptable, and able to learn something valuable from every single experience.

The parallels between that childhood bike crash and adult life are seriously eye-opening. Both involve plans and expectations that often go completely sideways. Both require split-second adaptability when circumstances change. Both teach us that protection (whether helmets or emotional safeguards) matters, but can never prevent every bump and bruise. Both remind us that while we can't control every variable, we absolutely can control how we respond when things go wrong.

Maybe most importantly, both show us that sometimes the most direct path—that steep downhill route—isn't always the safest or most beneficial in the long run. Detours, though they might initially seem like frustrating delays, often hold unexpected gifts: beautiful views we would have missed, connections with people we wouldn't have otherwise met, lessons we couldn't have learned any other way.

In this chapter, we're diving into life's roller coaster, exploring the detours we face and the incredible lessons they teach us. We'll look at personal crises, global events, and significant milestones, like turning 40 and taking stock of our lives. These disruptions, though challenging, can lead to remarkable growth and self-discovery. So let's jump into this journey together, embracing the unexpected and uncovering the hidden wisdom in life's detours and discoveries.

The Unexpected Curveball

If there's one thing I've learned over the years, it's that life is wildly unpredictable. Just when you think you've got everything figured out, it throws you a curveball that leaves you completely spinning.

2016 was, hands down, a life-landmark year for me. One of those pivotal moments you simply can't erase from your memory, no matter how hard you try. At the time, I was happily remarried, had a job I loved, and everything seemed to be going perfectly. But then, life decided it was time for things to get real.

It started with a completely ordinary phone call from

my daughter's school, letting me know she had a headache. Nothing unusual there, right? Little did I know that headache would mark the beginning of a multi-year battle with Anti-NMDA Receptor Encephalitis. If you're scratching your head wondering "what in the world is anti-nmda receptor encephalitis?"—try living with it for several years! Suddenly, the life I had known completely vanished. My family was shaken to the core, and my husband and I became full-time caregivers to our precious girl, who sometimes couldn't even recognize us. It was, without question, the most challenging period of my entire life.

That phone call represents a moment many of us have experienced—that unexpected turning point that divides life into "before" and "after." It seemed so innocent at first: just a child with a headache, a routine call from the school nurse. These are the everyday disruptions parents handle all the time without thinking twice. But this call marked the beginning of a journey none of us could have possibly anticipated or prepared for.

Anti-NMDA Receptor Encephalitis—the words themselves sound clinical, distant, almost abstract. The reality was anything but. It's an autoimmune disease that happens when antibodies produced by the body's own immune system attack NMDA receptors in the brain. These receptors play a crucial role in memory formation, learning, and behavior. When they're compromised, every aspect of a person's functioning can be affected: movement, speech, memory, personality, even the ability to recognize loved ones.

For my daughter, this meant a rapid descent from normal adolescent life into a bewildering world of medical interventions, hospital stays, and profound cognitive disruption.

For our family, it meant navigating an incredibly complex medical maze while watching our vibrant child struggle with basic functions, sometimes looking at us with absolutely no recognition in her eyes. The pain of that moment—when your child looks at you as if you're a complete stranger—is impossible to describe. It cuts to the very core of your identity as a parent, challenging the fundamental belief that you'll always be able to protect your child, that they'll always know you as their safe place.

Yet, in the middle of that enormous detour, I somehow found the strength to make significant changes. I quit my job, started a small business, and launched a nonprofit for girls and women. It's amazing how life has a way of pulling purpose from the depths of pain and tragedy. I could go into all the details of that journey, but honestly, that story deserves its own book.

This transformation didn't happen overnight or without serious struggle. The decision to leave my job wasn't made lightly—it came after countless nights trying to balance workplace demands with hospital visits, after too many moments of being physically present but mentally a million miles away, after realizing that my daughter's condition required a level of attention and advocacy that simply wasn't compatible with my previous professional commitments.

Starting a business in the middle of such personal chaos might seem completely backwards, but it provided something essential: flexibility and a sense of purpose I could control when everything else felt like it was spiraling. The nonprofit grew from watching my daughter struggle with identity and self-esteem issues during her illness and recovery—seeing firsthand how crucial support networks are for girls and women facing life's challenges. What began as a response to personal crisis evolved into a mission to ensure other young women had resources I wished had been available to my daughter.

Looking back, I sometimes wonder how my daughter and I made it through that ordeal. I get those social media memories with images of her and me, our family taking turns at the hospital. The complete turbulence of unknowns and even facing that terrifying space of potentially losing someone so incredibly close to my heart. I honestly didn't think we would make it out alive or with any clarity of mind. But here's the thing: we did. And that's a testament to the resilience and adaptability we all possess when faced with life's most significant detours.

The resilience we discovered wasn't superhuman or extraordinary—it was built day by day, moment by moment, through countless small acts of perseverance. It was found in the hospital room dance parties we held when my daughter had a good day. It was in the way my husband and I would tag-team care responsibilities, making sure one of us was always present while allowing the other brief moments to recharge. It was in the unexpected kindnesses from nurses who became like family, from friends who showed up with home-cooked meals, from colleagues who covered work responsibilities without being asked.

As I navigated through that unexpected detour, I began to realize that life is full of twists and turns, often taking us to places we never could have imagined. What I initially saw as a massive setback was actually an opportunity for growth, self-discovery, and a chance to completely redefine my priorities.

This perspective shift didn't happen right away. It emerged

gradually as I witnessed small victories in my daughter's recovery—the first time she recognized me again after weeks of confusion, the moment she laughed at a familiar joke, the day she held a conversation for more than a few minutes. Each tiny step forward revealed that progress wasn't linear but cumulative, that healing happened on its own timeline rather than according to our preferred schedule.

During that period of complete uncertainty, I found comfort in connecting with others who had faced similar challenges. Their stories of strength and courage inspired me to keep pushing forward, even when the odds seemed completely stacked against us. I used to drive past the hospital and think to myself how unfortunate those families were until I became one of them. I became more empathetic, more understanding, and more deeply connected to the struggles that others face.

This newfound empathy was another unexpected gift from this difficult detour. Before my daughter's illness, I could acknowledge others' suffering intellectually but couldn't truly understand the day-to-day reality of navigating a serious medical condition. Afterward, I understood the weight of uncertainty, the exhaustion of constant vigilance, the way a medical crisis affects absolutely every aspect of family life. This deeper understanding changed how I relate to others in crisis—less advice, more presence; fewer platitudes, more practical support; less judgment, more grace.

The experience also taught me about the incredible power of community and the importance of leaning on each other during tough times. It was through the support of friends, family, and even complete strangers that I found the strength to keep going and eventually triumph over adversity.

Finding Light in Darkness

Life has a way of throwing serious curveballs, and it's an inescapable reality that we'll all face our fair share of storms. But let me tell you something important—even in the darkest moments, there are always rays of sunshine that break through the clouds. In the middle of all that chaos, my family welcomed the most beautiful blessing: my son Jayce, whose name literally means "to be healed." His arrival reminded us that there's always hope, even in the most trying times.

Jayce's birth during this incredibly challenging period wasn't just a happy coincidence—it was a profound reminder of life's continuous cycle of renewal and possibility. While one child was fighting to reclaim her health, another was beginning his journey, bringing with him all the promise and potential that a new life represents. His name—meaning "to be healed"—wasn't chosen randomly but as a declaration of faith in restoration, not just for my daughter but for our entire family.

There's something uniquely powerful about holding a newborn while sitting beside a hospital bed. The contrast creates a perspective that few experiences can match—the vulnerability of both beginning and threatened life, the precious fragility of our existence, the remarkable resilience of the human body in both states. Jayce became our family's living reminder that even in seasons of intense struggle, new beginnings are possible, that joy and sorrow can coexist, that healing comes in many forms.

And speaking of silver linings, my daughter was granted a Make-a-Wish trip to Disney World! Picture our entire squad—a lively, motley crew—hitting up Disney, Sea World, and Universal Studios. It was absolutely magical, and we had the time of our lives. Those moments of pure joy and togetherness reminded us that there's still so much to be grateful for, even when life is throwing its worst at you.

Ultimately, I've come to understand that it's not the storms that define our lives, but how we respond to them. We can choose to dwell on the darkness or search for the light, embracing the lessons and growth that come from life's challenges.

This perspective isn't about toxic positivity or denying the reality of suffering. It's about developing a mindset that acknowledges pain while refusing to be defined by it. It's about recognizing that while we can't always choose our circumstances, we can choose our response to them. It's about understanding that even the most difficult experiences contain the seeds of growth, wisdom, and deepened capacity for empathy if we're willing to look for them.

Pandemic Pivots

You can't say 'twenty-twenty' without thinking about that global pothole that hit everyone in completely different ways. For me, the world came to a screeching halt, and life as I knew it changed dramatically. I went from being a motivational speaker, traveling all over, to being a homeschool teacher at what I like to call "The Cray-Cray Academy"—and let me tell you, it was quite the ride! Businesses closed their doors, and everything outside our home made life feel so confined. Fear became a constant companion, and anxiety was never far behind.

The pandemic was a unique kind of detour—one we all experienced collectively yet individually. While everyone faced the same global crisis, our particular challenges were shaped by our specific circumstances: family setup, work requirements, health vulnerabilities, access to resources, and countless other factors. My transition from motivational speaker to homeschool teacher wasn't one I would have chosen, but it was one that millions of parents worldwide were suddenly navigating alongside me.

"The Cray-Cray Academy" emerged out of pure necessity, with a curriculum developed on the fly and teaching credentials consisting mainly of patience, creativity, and an occasionally questionable sense of humor. Our classroom wasn't equipped with state-of-the-art technology or carefully designed learning stations. It was our dining table, cleared of breakfast dishes and covered with hastily printed worksheets, makeshift science experiments, and art supplies that somehow managed to migrate to every surface of our home.

I never thought I'd be the kind of mom who homeschooled her kids, but life had other plans. And while I won't lie and say it was all sunshine and rainbows, I will admit that it taught me a lot about patience, resilience, and the importance of finding humor in the most challenging situations. I can't forget the impromptu dance parties in between math problems because sometimes, you just need to shake off the stress and have a little fun.

Those dance parties weren't just breaks from academics—they were essential mental health interventions for both my children and myself. They became our way of physically releasing tension, of reminding ourselves that joy was still possible even in confinement, of connecting through movement when words felt inadequate to express the strangeness of our new reality. What began as a spontaneous coping mechanism evolved into a deliberate practice, a way of punctuating our days with moments of uninhibited happiness amid the uncertainty.

The pandemic wasn't just about educational adjustments, though. It fundamentally altered our sense of safety, our social connections, our relationship with public spaces, and our perception of time itself. Days blurred together in what many called "pandemic time"—a strange elongation of moments that somehow also accelerated months. Traditional markers of seasons and celebrations were disrupted, creating a disorienting experience of life without the usual rhythms and rituals.

But the pandemic wasn't the only thing that changed my life.

You know, life's a funny thing. It's filled with ups and downs, twists and turns, and moments that can make or break us. But in the midst of it all, there's always something to learn, a reason to hope, and a way to find the light – even when it seems like the darkness is never-ending.

Education as an Anchor

As if everything wasn't hectic enough, I decided to enroll in college to pursue a master's degree. Despite my less-than-stellar homeschooling attempts, I was determined to succeed in my academic journey. After all, I've always been a lifelong learner, eager to push my limits and see just how far I can go. I didn't take the traditional route to my bachelor's, but that didn't stop me. Whenever life feels like it's spinning out of control, I search for the things I can control – and for me, that's education.

The decision to pursue higher education during a global pandemic while homeschooling multiple children might seem completely insane, even reckless. But for me, academia offered something precious amid chaos: structure, intellectual engagement, and measurable progress. While so much of life felt suspended in uncertainty, coursework provided clear expectations, definable goals, and tangible achievements. In a world where we couldn't control a virus's spread or predict when normal life might resume, I could control how much I studied, when I completed assignments, and how thoroughly I engaged with the material.

Education has always served as one of my anchors during turbulent times—not as an escape from reality but as a way of making sense of it, of developing frameworks to understand complex experiences, of connecting my personal challenges to broader human questions. Each course became not just an academic requirement but a lens through which to interpret what was happening around me, a tool for creating meaning from disruption.

The practical logistics of pursuing a master's degree while managing a household during a pandemic required creativity and compromise. Late nights became my sanctuary for reading and writing after children were finally asleep. Early mornings transformed into precious windows for focused thought before the day's demands began. Car rides (even just to pick up groceries) turned into mobile classrooms as I listened to recorded lectures. What might have seemed like impossible time constraints became an exercise in finding hidden pockets of opportunity within each day.

As I was nearing the finish line of my master's program, life threw us another curveball. My daughter, who had so bravely battled that rare form of encephalitis, started experiencing anxiety and fatigue. We initially thought it was just a lingering cold, but after she fainted at school and collapsed again in my bedroom, we knew something more serious was happening.

After rushing her to the emergency room, we discovered that she had a pulmonary embolism and blood clots in her lungs – a complication from the port she had for infusions during her encephalitis treatment. Our hearts broke as we listened to the doctors explain the severity of her condition and the long road to recovery that lay ahead. It was a stark reminder that life can change in an instant, and we must cherish every moment we have with our loved ones.

This medical emergency represented a particularly cruel twist—complications arising from the very treatment that had saved her life during her previous illness. The port that had delivered life-sustaining medications had now created a life-threatening condition of its own. It was as if we had successfully navigated one treacherous mountain pass only to discover another, equally dangerous one just beyond. The unfairness of it threatened to overwhelm us—hadn't she already endured enough? Hadn't our family been tested sufficiently?

Yet even this setback contained unexpected gifts. The previous experience with serious illness had equipped us with invaluable knowledge—how to advocate effectively within medical systems, how to communicate clearly with healthcare providers, how to balance necessary vigilance with equally necessary rest. The coping skills we had developed during her encephalitis treatment weren't lost but were immediately available, like muscles that had been strengthened through previous use. We were still afraid, still heartbroken, but no longer novices in navigating medical crises.

But, as I've learned time and time again, there's always

sunshine after the rain. Our girl fought her way back and not even two months later, our entire family – including my brave girl – traveled to Tulsa, Oklahoma, to watch me graduate with my master's degree, top of my class, and even earn the Outstanding Student of the Year Award. It was a moment of triumph, a celebration of our collective resilience, and proof that we can rise above and find the light even in the face of adversity.

That graduation ceremony transcended the typical academic milestone. It became a family victory, a testament to what's possible when we support each other through challenges. Having my daughter there—the same child who had been hospitalized just weeks earlier—wasn't just personally meaningful; it was symbolically powerful. Her presence embodied the very resilience my education had helped me articulate theoretically, creating a beautiful convergence of academic learning and lived experience.

The Outstanding Student award wasn't just recognition of academic performance but acknowledgment of the extraordinary circumstances under which that performance had been achieved. It validated the late nights, the creative time management, the unwavering determination to continue learning even when life seemed determined to interrupt that process. Most importantly, it confirmed something I had always believed but sometimes doubted during the hardest moments: that our challenges don't have to define our limits unless we allow them to.

Life's detours and discoveries have taught me that, through it all, we must remain steadfast in our pursuit of personal growth and hold on to the hope that there's always something beautiful waiting for us just around the corner. And as we navigate this unpredictable journey, we can find comfort in knowing that our experiences – both the good and the bad – are shaping us into the people we are meant to be.

Storms and Sunshine

As we continued to move forward, embracing the detours and discoveries life had thrown our way, I began to understand that every experience, no matter how challenging, was an opportunity for growth and transformation. And as I looked back on the years, I realized just how much I'd learned from these moments of uncertainty, pain, and joy.

I started to see that it wasn't just about surviving the storm but learning to dance in the rain. It was about understanding that life isn't meant to be a straight line, but rather a beautiful, winding path filled with unexpected twists and turns. And it was about recognizing that each detour presented a new opportunity to learn, to grow, and to become a better version of ourselves.

This perspective shift represents one of the most profound gifts of navigating life's disruptions—the realization that the detours aren't interruptions to our journey but essential components of it. The unexpected turns aren't taking us off track but are actually creating the track itself, forming a path that is uniquely ours precisely because of its irregularities and surprises. What initially appears as disruption often reveals itself as direction when viewed with sufficient perspective.

I also found that by sharing my experiences with others, I could inspire and encourage those who were facing their own challenges. My story, though unique to me, was a testament to the power of resilience, hope, and faith. I discovered that the things I'd gone through weren't meant for me to hold onto, but rather to share with others as a source of strength and inspiration.

This discovery—that our struggles take on new meaning when shared—transformed how I viewed my most difficult experiences. What once seemed like senseless suffering began to reveal purpose when it helped someone else navigate their own dark moments. The vulnerability required to share authentically became not a weakness but a powerful connection point, a way of transforming personal pain into communal wisdom.

As I continued to share my story, I started to see the incredible impact it could have on those around me. I watched as people found hope in the midst of their darkest moments, as they embraced their own detours and discovered the strength within themselves to keep moving forward. And it was in these moments that I realized my purpose – to use my experiences to empower others, to encourage them to rise above their circumstances, and to help them find the beauty in life's unexpected detours.

Writing Through Storms

As I began writing this book during the pandemic, it felt like I was trapped in a relentless hailstorm of life's tumultuous events. My baby brother, who is four years my junior, suffered a heart attack on an airplane right in front of my horrified niece and nephew. By some divine intervention, a heart doctor happened to be on the same flight and managed to save his life. That same year, my paternal grandmother passed away, and due to circumstances beyond my control, I couldn't attend her funeral. The lingering pain of not being able to say "goodbye" still haunts me, a heavy burden I continue to carry while also reminding myself to love the people in my life while they are here.

These concurrent crises created what psychologists call "compound trauma"—multiple significant stressors occurring simultaneously or in quick succession, giving the psyche insufficient time to process one event before confronting another. The heart attack that nearly took my brother, the grandmother's passing that I couldn't properly mourn, the ongoing pandemic restrictions that amplified every loss by disrupting normal grieving rituals—each alone would have been challenging, but together they created an overwhelming convergence of emotional demands.

The storm intensified as it reached my doorstep when an early morning phone call informed me that my 17-year-old son had been arrested. I was told he would be released the next day, but reality proved otherwise. Suddenly, I was thrust into a world of uncertainty and desperation, where my only contact with my son was a brief 15 minutes per day, if that, on a recorded line. In those precious moments, I tried my hardest to encourage him not to lose hope. With the horrifying images of George Floyd's murder and the subsequent racial injustice fresh in my mind, I was terrified that my son might be charged as an adult. Each day, I prayed and cried for his safe return, grappling with feelings of helplessness and despair.

My son's arrest represented a particularly complex intersection of personal crisis and societal context. It occurred amid heightened awareness of racial disparities in the justice system following George Floyd's murder and the national reckoning it prompted. This timing added layers of fear beyond the already terrifying experience of having a child in custody—fear informed by too many stories of Black youth receiving harsher treatment, being denied due process, or experiencing violence within the system. Each day of separation wasn't just about missing my son but about fighting against the paralysis of these larger fears while maintaining hope and practical advocacy.

These moments of hopelessness are forever etched in my memory, but it's essential to acknowledge the one thing that held me together: my unwavering faith in God. Through all the trials and tribulations, it was His grace and guidance that gave me the strength to persevere and eventually share these experiences with you. My faith became my anchor, steadying me in the stormy seas of life's challenges. As I look back on those dark days, I realize that I emerged from the storm stronger, more resilient, and with a deeper understanding of life's complexities. And it is my hope that by sharing my story, you too can find the strength to navigate life's detours and discover the light that shines through even the darkest of times.

Faith in this context wasn't about simple answers or magical resolution of problems. It wasn't about believing everything would turn out exactly as I hoped or that suffering would be immediately alleviated. Rather, it provided a framework for making meaning from seemingly senseless events, a source of strength when personal reserves were depleted, and a reminder that even in isolation, I was not ultimately alone. Faith offered not certainty but sustenance—the spiritual equivalent of bread for the journey, enough to take the next step even when the entire path remained obscured.

Milestone Reflections
Since the first edition of this book, I've found myself

winding through a seemingly infinite labyrinth of detours and discoveries. As I crossed that milestone of turning 40, I was hit with a tidal wave of reflections, prompting me to reevaluate just how precious my time truly is. It got me wondering what my life had amounted to so far and questioning how much sand remained in my hourglass. Mortality decided to cozy up and take center stage in my thoughts, and while I wouldn't dare label it a midlife crisis, there's no doubt that it rattled my worldview.

Turning 40 represents one of life's significant threshold moments—a cultural milestone that prompts questions about identity, purpose, and legacy regardless of one's particular circumstances. For me, this birthday coincided with an unusual period of global uncertainty and personal challenge, amplifying its impact. The questions that arose weren't simply about age but about meaning: What truly matters? How do I want to spend whatever time remains? What legacy am I creating through my choices? What parts of my life align with my deepest values, and what parts might need recalibration?

All at once, the allure of social media and the compulsion to post every little detail of my life lost its luster. I chose to embark on a season of intentional isolation, using that time to excavate the depths of my existence and identify what genuinely mattered to me. And you know what? It was while navigating these very detours and discoveries that I came to realize they were the chisel and hammer that had carefully crafted me into the person I am today – a person I'm not just content with, but downright proud to be.

This digital detox represented more than just a break from social platforms; it signified a fundamental shift in how I related to my own experiences. Without the reflexive urge to document and share every moment, I found myself more fully present in each experience. Without the subtle but persistent influence of others' curated lives, I could more clearly discern my authentic preferences and priorities. Without the dopamine hits of external validation through likes and comments, I rediscovered internal sources of satisfaction and meaning.

The isolation wasn't about withdrawal from meaningful connection but about creating space to hear my own voice more clearly. It was about distinguishing between the noise of cultural expectations and the quieter signals of personal purpose. It was about recognizing which aspects of my identity were authentic expressions of my values and which were performative responses to external pressures. This clarity didn't emerge instantly but gradually, like a landscape revealing itself as fog slowly lifts.

During this period of introspection, I discovered that life isn't just about the wins and the losses, but rather the lessons we learn from each twist and turn. I began to see that my experiences, both good and bad, had given me a unique perspective and a wealth of wisdom to share with others. The things I once considered setbacks were, in fact, building blocks for my personal growth.

This reframing represents one of the most powerful shifts possible in human perspective—the ability to see challenges not merely as obstacles to happiness but as essential components of development. It doesn't deny the real pain of difficult experiences or suggest that suffering is somehow desirable. Rather, it acknowledges that our capacity for growth, wisdom, and empathy is often expanded precisely through the experiences we would never choose but must navigate nonetheless.

So, I embraced this newfound understanding and allowed it to guide me in my journey. I started paying more attention to the people and experiences that truly enriched my life and let go of the things that didn't serve my purpose. I took risks, pursued passions, and most importantly, I kept growing.

Now, as I continue to navigate this roller coaster we call life, I can't help but feel grateful for every detour and discovery that has led me to this very moment. And as I share my story with you, it is my hope that it will not only inspire and encourage you but also remind you that, regardless of the storms we face, there's always sunshine waiting to break through the clouds.

Why Our Unfiltered Stories Matter Most

Let me take you into my writer-mind for a moment. Okay, can we talk about *Romancing the Stone* for a second? I'm about to date myself here, but I don't even care. When I first watched that movie, I wasn't just captivated by Michael Douglas's rugged charm (though, hello!). I was completely obsessed with Kathleen Turner's character—this romance novelist who literally cried while typing the final scenes of her own book.

I wanted that. Not the crying part necessarily (though who hasn't sobbed over their own words at some point?), but that deep, soul-stirring connection to your craft. That magical moment where you're so immersed in your own creation that you forget where you end and your characters begin.

In my mind, that was the dream. I'd picture myself in some gorgeous apartment (way nicer than anything I could actually afford), dramatically typing away with perfect hair (also unrealistic) and producing these incredible stories that would make readers swoon. What my sweet, naive self didn't realize was that Joan Wilder wasn't manufacturing emotion—she was tapping into something real and raw within herself.

That image stuck with me for years, becoming the gold

standard I measured my own writing against. But here's what the movie montage didn't show: the doubt-filled 3 AM staring contests with a blank page, the rejection letters that feel like personal attacks, or the way criticism can make you question every life choice that led you to put words on paper. They don't show you the courage it takes to put your heart on the page, knowing someone might just shrug and say, "Meh."

Let's be honest—if they showed the real writer's life, it would have been a silent film, not a romance!

But as I stumbled (sometimes gracefully, often not) through my own writing journey, I discovered something powerful: stories connect us in ways nothing else can. They bridge impossible gaps and help us see each other—really see each other. But here's the kicker—for stories to have that magic, they need realness and vulnerability. Not just a sprinkle, but all of it.

And you know what makes a story stick with you long after the book closes or the credits roll? It's not fancy plot twists or perfect prose (though those don't hurt). It's emotional truth. It's that moment of recognition when you think, "Oh my gosh, I've felt that too!" even if the character's life looks nothing like yours. That's the real magic.

The Courage of Vulnerability

One of the things I've learned the hard way is that being vulnerable is terrifying—like standing in your underwear during a job interview. We all want to package ourselves neatly, showing only our highlight reel while the blooper reel stays safely hidden in some password-protected folder of our hearts.

I get it! Vulnerability feels like handing someone a baseball bat, telling them to swing, and hoping they don't aim at your softest parts. There's nothing irrational about that fear—we've all had those moments when we shared something real only to have it tossed back in our faces like confetti at a breakup party.

Maybe you spilled your guts about a dream only to have someone roll their eyes and call it "unrealistic." Perhaps you admitted a mistake and then had it weaponized against you six months later in an argument about something totally unrelated. Or you shared an opinion that wasn't popular and suddenly found yourself eating lunch alone.

Those experiences teach us to build walls higher than my credit card bill after "therapeutic Amazon shopping." We learn to filter, edit, and present only the most Instagram-worthy versions of ourselves. The problem? That strategy might protect us from pain, but it also blocks us from the deep connections that make life worth living.

Think about the books, movies, or conversations that have knocked the wind out of you (in the best way). I'm willing to bet my favorite pair of pumps they weren't the ones with perfect characters living perfect lives with perfect hair. They were the messy ones, the stories that dove headfirst into the complicated, sometimes awful parts of being human.

The stories that cling to our souls are the ones that feel TRUE—not because they're factual, but because they capture something essential about living in these weird human bodies with our weird human hearts. They show characters with mixed motives, making terrible decisions for understandable reasons, being both incredibly brave and frustratingly cowardly within the same chapter—you know, just like us actual humans.

When someone shares their unfiltered truth, it's like they've handed you a permission slip to acknowledge your own messy reality. That sigh of relief you feel? It's the sound of realizing you're not the only disaster in progress, not uniquely flawed or broken beyond repair. It's the "me too" moment that makes you feel less alone in your struggles.

This is why the stories that punch us in the feelings usually come from the author's most vulnerable places. They're not written to show off or preach—they're written to make sense of their own experiences, to find the thread of meaning running through the chaos, to transform their wounds into wisdom. When we read these stories, we're not just consuming content; we're participating in a sacred exchange that heals both the teller and the listener.

One-Sided Stories and Half-Truths

I was the QUEEN of one-sided stories growing up. Seriously, if there had been an Olympic event for creative blame-shifting, I would have taken gold, silver, AND bronze. It was always someone else's fault, even if there wasn't actually anyone else around. The devil made me do it? Amateur hour. I'd blame my imaginary friend, my little brother, or the family cat with Academy Award-worthy conviction.

And Mom, if you're reading this…it was me.

But here's the thing—that childhood habit of telling stories that make us look good doesn't magically disappear when we grow up. We just get more sophisticated about it. We no longer blame imaginary friends, but we definitely curate our social media to show only our victories and filter our anecdotes depending on which version makes us look best in the current company.

These one-sided stories aren't necessarily lies. They're just... selective truths. The problem is, when we only tell partial truths, we prevent genuine connection. People might admire our highlight reel, but they can't truly know us. They might sympathize with our victim stories, but they can't authentically support our growth beyond victimhood.

As I wrote this book, I caught myself doing this exact thing—crafting these pretty, Pinterest-worthy stories that made me look thoughtful and wise and evolved. But something felt off. These stories were true, but they weren't the WHOLE truth. They weren't stories that would help you see yourself more clearly because I wasn't being clear about myself.

This was a major lightbulb moment for me. I realized I was still that kid blaming her imaginary friend—just with better vocabulary and more strategic omissions. I was crafting narratives that protected my ego instead of serving the deeper purpose of connection.

As we journey through this book together, I promise to keep it real—the good, the bad, and the "oh honey, what were you thinking?" Because those unfiltered stories are the ones that truly connect us and remind us that we're all just figuring this life thing out as we go.

Beyond the Highlight Reel

Can we talk about social media for a second? That carefully curated world where everyone's living their best life 24/7? Where marriages are perfect, children are always well-behaved, work is fulfilling, and apparently, no one ever has spinach in their teeth or a zit on picture day?

It's exhausting. And it's also complete nonsense.

This highlight-reel epidemic isn't just an influencer thing—

it's embedded in our everyday interactions. We ask, "How are you?" but send all kinds of subtle signals that we expect the standard "Fine, thanks" rather than "Actually, I'm struggling to get out of bed, and I can't remember if I fed my kids breakfast or just dreamed that I did." We've collectively created social norms that reward performance over being real, and we're all paying the price in disconnection.

When we share our unfiltered stories—the ones with messy emotions and imperfect outcomes—we're not just opening up about our challenges. We're creating space for others to exhale and think, "Oh thank goodness, it's not just me." That relief can be life-changing. It's the difference between thinking you're the only one struggling and realizing you're part of a community of imperfect humans just trying to figure things out.

Learning Through Stumbling

Let me tell you about one of my most cringe-worthy moments. I was invited to perform at this fancy annual event in my city—a big deal, especially since I'd performed the year before and was thrilled to be asked back. I rehearsed like crazy and even splurged on a new outfit (because priorities, right?).

The day arrived, and I was taking my sweet time getting ready. Why rush when you're basically a professional at this point? Then the phone rang. It was the event organizers asking if I was on my way.

"Of course," I said confidently, assuring them I'd be there shortly.

Plot twist: I was the opening act. And the program had already started. WITHOUT ME.

I frantically threw myself together and raced to the venue,

only to be greeted by a room full of stone-faced people who were clearly not impressed with my tardiness. I stumbled through my two songs with all the grace of a newborn giraffe and then slunk off to the corner to hide with my husband, completely mortified.

For years, I carried this story as a private shame, occasionally telling a version where miscommunication was the villain. But the honest truth? I hadn't confirmed the time. I'd assumed. And we all know what happens when we assume. (We end up performing badly in front of a room full of annoyed people, that's what.)

That humiliating experience taught me something invaluable about the importance of clear communication and double-checking details. To this day, I have approximately 17 reminders set when I'm supposed to be somewhere important because that kind of public embarrassment is not something you want to experience twice.

Whew! I've been holding that story in for YEARS! Telling it in all its unfiltered glory feels surprisingly freeing. It allows me to own my mistake rather than crafting a narrative where I was just a victim of circumstances.

The Reality of Expectations

Want another cringe-worthy confession? Let's talk about my first book. Y'all, I was SO ready for my literary debut. I'd poured my heart and soul into those pages, revealing my deepest thoughts and most vulnerable experiences. With my solid social media following, I just knew success was inevitable. I could practically see my name on bestseller lists and hear the ping of endless notification alerts as sales rolled in.

Reality check: those sales didn't exactly come flooding in.

Instead of congratulatory messages and glowing reviews, I got… crickets. The deafening kind. I'd seriously overestimated the demand for my book.

And let me tell you, that box of unsold books sitting in my garage—my life stories, my heart work—staring back at me was a gut punch of epic proportions. Each copy seemed to whisper, "Not good enough" on repeat like the world's most demotivating soundtrack. It's the kind of disappointment that makes you question everything about yourself and your abilities.

But here's the thing—that setback didn't break me. It bruised my ego (significantly), but it also forced me to take a step back and reevaluate. I realized my expectations were rooted in fear—the fear of not being enough. I was seeking validation through book sales instead of writing from a place of genuine service and connection.

As I processed the disappointment, I shifted my perspective from external validation to internal satisfaction. I found joy in the process of creating rather than obsessing over outcomes. It was surprisingly liberating to let go of the pressure to please everyone and instead focus on the readers who did connect with my words.

Looking back, I see that this painful experience was actually a detour that led me to discover the true value of my writing. If even one person finds comfort or inspiration in my words, I've accomplished what matters most.

The Gift of Simply Being Real

So what does it really mean to share our unfiltered stories? It means being raw, honest, and transparent about our lives—the triumphs AND the face-plants. It means digging deep and sharing the moments that have shaped us, even when it's uncomfortable. It means being brave enough to say, "This is me, imperfections and all," and trusting that your vulnerability will create a space for others to do the same.

This kind of transparent sharing isn't about attention-seeking or collecting sympathy points. It's about creating genuine connections through our shared humanity. When we offer our unfiltered stories, we're essentially saying, "This is what being human looks like for me. Does any of this resonate with you?" We're starting a conversation rather than performing a monologue.

The gift of being real extends in all directions. When we share our unfiltered stories, we offer others the validation of knowing they're not alone. We create permission for them to acknowledge their own challenges. We demonstrate that imperfection isn't something to hide but something to integrate into a fuller understanding of ourselves.

But realness is also a gift we give ourselves. When we commit to honest self-expression, we release the exhausting burden of maintaining facades. We create space for genuine self-acceptance and growth. We align our outer presentation with our inner reality, reducing the cognitive dissonance that contributes to so much of our stress.

Don't shy away from sharing your full story—the highlights AND the bloopers. Embrace your beautiful mess, and know that your unfiltered truth is your greatest gift to a world drowning in perfectionism. Your story matters—not despite its imperfections, but because of them.

In the end, it's not about having a perfect story, but about embracing the journey with all its unexpected plot twists. By sharing our unfiltered tales, we help others find comfort in their own struggles and remember that none of us have it all figured out. And together, we can navigate this unpredictable, messy, and beautiful thing called life—one authentic story at a time.

Sweet Surrender

Friends, I have to make a tiny confession. Here it is: I firmly believe in Vision Boards. Wait, I *used* to. Let me explain.

Vision boards are amazing for keeping your goals front and center in your life. I still think they have their place. But somewhere between carefully cutting out magazine pictures and arranging them on poster board, I learned a powerful lesson about the massive gap between visualizing something and actually doing the work to make it happen.

And let me rush to clarify—I'm on the non-manifesting, non-crystal-rubbing, non-praying-to-the-universe train. It's all faith in God for me. No shade to the sage burners, but that life isn't my jam. I need something a little more substantial than good vibes when my pants don't button.

For the longest time, I had this affirmation I would declare with complete conviction: "I am in the best shape of my life." I even added a bonus statement that should have been my first red flag: "I can eat anything I want because I am in the best shape of my life."

Remember those unfiltered tales I promised? Buckle up for another one.

The Pancake Love Affair That Once Was

I used to LOVE pancakes. Not just a casual, "Oh, pancakes are nice" kind of love. I'm talking deep, profound, write-a-song-about-it LOVE. And not just any pancakes—the light and fluffy ones where butter melts into every single crevice and warm maple syrup cascades down those golden-brown sides like a sweet waterfall. The ones with pecans nestled throughout the batter, creating little pockets of nutty goodness that surprise your taste buds. The ones studded with plump blueberries that burst with sweetness, topped with a dollop of freshly whipped cream that slowly melts into creamy rivulets.

Just typing that paragraph made me seriously consider stopping right now to whip up a batch. That's how serious this relationship was to me.

I'll admit when I was desperate, I'd even grab hotcakes from McDonald's, though I have to admit—I don't eat a single thing from that menu anymore. (Don't judge me; we've all been there at some point!)

My love for pancakes didn't just grow during quarantine; it expanded into something approaching spiritual devotion. Like, "Should I start a pancake-based religion?" level of dedication. Pancake-ianity? The Church of Latter-Day Flapjacks? I haven't worked out the details but you get where this was going.

The Miracle of Motivation (While It Lasted)

My vision board was working PERFECTLY for me about a week after welcoming my newest blessing, Jaxon. Motivation coursed through my veins as I prepared to compete in a pageant. I was walking every single day, sometimes twice, and working out every night after the house quieted down.

Like some kind of postpartum miracle, my body bounced back with remarkable speed!

Can you hear me? I was in complete snapback mode AND still enjoying a perfectly fluffy pancake each morning. Life was good. No, life was GREAT. I was living the dream—having my pancake and eating it too!

After the pageant concluded (and yes, I did well, thank you for asking), I began scaling back on my fitness regimen. I reasoned with myself, "Hey, why not loosen up a little? You've earned it." My discipline loosened as I convinced myself I didn't need to maintain such rigorous workouts. After all, the evidence was clear—I was literally in the best shape of my life. The mirror told me so. My clothes told me so. My affirmations DEFINITELY told me so.

The Slippery Slope of Seasonal Excuses

Then something predictable yet somehow surprising happened—the weather started changing. The crisp fall air made outdoor walks less appealing. The early sunsets cut my available daylight hours. The occasional drizzle provided the perfect excuse to stay inside where it was warm and cozy.

Me? No problem at all. I'll simply make it up with an extra at-home workout. I bought new resistance bands. Downloaded fitness apps. Subscribed to online workout platforms.

Only that didn't actually happen.

What happened instead was me sitting on my couch, scrolling through workout videos, mentally calculating if I could complete them while simultaneously not moving a single muscle. "That looks doable," I'd think, as I reached for another snack. The only six-pack I was developing was in my Amazon cart—resistance bands I'd never use.

Thanksgiving arrived with its annual parade of culinary temptations. As the designated family chef, I had to make all the traditional favorites: velvety mashed potatoes swimming in butter, creamy mac and cheese, moist cornbread that crumbles just right, savory dressing (and by that, I mean stuffing, though we'll debate that terminology another time), candied yams, brussels sprouts glazed with my special sauce and generous bacon bits, and a spiral ham glistening with brown sugar glaze. All of it made with love, butter, and more butter.

By that point, workouts had faded into a pleasant but distant memory, something I'd definitely return to... someday... perhaps when the stars aligned perfectly. Christmas followed with its cookie exchanges, festive dinners, and endless treats. Old Man Winter didn't just bring cold weather; he dragged along several pounds that somehow attached themselves to my midsection, thighs, and even my once-defined arms.

Through all these seasonal changes, I remained loyal to one constant companion—my beloved pancakes. In the immortal words of Effie from "Dreamgirls": "No. No. No. Noooooooooooo way! Never living without you!" I might've sung this to my plate on more than one occasion. The neighbors probably thought I was serenading my husband, but nope—just professing my undying love to breakfast food.

My Vendetta Against the Bathroom Scale

Something rather peculiar began happening, though. I don't recall pancakes previously causing side effects like developing a vendetta against my bathroom scale. I harbored such intense animosity toward this innocent measuring device that I found myself rolling my eyes dramatically whenever I encountered it during my bathroom visits.

I called it names—names I absolutely cannot repeat on these pages. The numbers it displayed had to be wrong. They simply didn't compute with my reality. So I made the executive decision to stop looking altogether.

The scale was obviously malfunctioning because my LuluLemon leggings still fit perfectly fine. If I needed to do a little extra wiggling to get them over my hips, well, that was clearly a manufacturing issue. The company must have changed their sizing without warning. It happens all the time, right?

There was absolutely no logical explanation for how I could consume a pancake daily without gaining an ounce a few months earlier, while now the scale kept flashing numbers I'd never seen associated with my body before. There had to be a technical glitch in the system, a cosmic error, perhaps even a small gravitational anomaly affecting only my bathroom floor.

My affirmations confirmed what I already knew—I was in the best shape of my life. I could eat whatever I wanted without consequences. That was my truth, and I was sticking to it like syrup to a pancake.

When Reality Comes Knocking

I recognized, in moments of uncomfortable clarity, that I was completely ignoring the persistent message screaming from my inner being. She was straight-up telling me, "Child, now you know good and well you cannot eat pancakes every single day, completely abandon your workouts, and somehow expect to lose weight or even maintain your current size."

But I wasn't trying to hear that wisdom. Fingers in ears. Nah Nah Nah Nah Nah! So there. Sometimes we choose delusion when reality becomes inconvenient. Actually, make that OFTEN we choose delusion when reality becomes inconvenient.

The truth was—and remains, despite my protests—I can absolutely eat pancakes and lose weight. I just have to skip all the ingredients that make pancakes worth eating: the butter, the syrup, the toppings. I'd need to craft some sad alternative from egg whites and protein powder that merely resembles a pancake in shape alone. And let's be honest—that's not a pancake. That's a disk-shaped protein vessel with pancake identity issues.

I'd also need to faithfully burn off those calories every day through consistent exercise, just as I had been doing during my disciplined phase. So maybe my scale wasn't the villain I'd made it out to be (though I didn't call it a "villain"—it was something much more colorful that would make this book need a parental advisory sticker).

It felt momentarily satisfying to direct my frustration at an inanimate object—until reality came crashing down when I attempted to put on my favorite pair of jeans. We won't even venture into that traumatic territory. Let's just say it involved lying on the bed, sucking in, and still not being able to zip them up. You know the drill. We've all performed the denim gymnastics at some point.

The Vision Without Action Problem

The vision board itself wasn't the culprit in this situation. It's genuinely valuable to articulate goals and display them prominently. Affirmations serve an important purpose in counteracting the negative thoughts that inevitably surface when we're pushing for meaningful change. They boost confidence when doubt creeps in.

My fundamental problem wasn't with these tools—it was believing that vision alone would manifest results without corresponding action. In the quieter, more honest corners of my mind, I knew this truth. I understood perfectly well that merely gazing at a vision board, no matter how beautifully crafted, wouldn't magically transform my body or my habits.

There's a common saying in personal development circles: "When you know better, you do better." That sounds wonderful in theory, but implementing it proves considerably more challenging. Despite watching my waistline steadily expand, despite struggling to climb stairs without getting winded, despite knowing intellectually that I needed to put down the pancakes and pick up the weights—I didn't. Knowledge didn't automatically translate into action. Awareness didn't guarantee change.

The Doctor's Office Reality Check

Then came the moment of reckoning—time for my annual doctor's visit. I scheduled a well-child checkup for my little one and made an appointment for myself to address an acne problem that had plagued me since puberty hit with full force.

This skin issue has been the persistent thorn in my flesh. One month my complexion might be gloriously clear and glowing; the next, angry inflamed bumps would erupt across my face, neck, and sometimes even my chest, appearing overnight like unwelcome guests who refuse to leave. But I digress from our main story.

I arrived for my appointment, they drew several vials of blood and ran a battery of standard tests. Thankfully, I received the acne prescription I had come seeking. However, as life often demonstrates, you don't always get exactly what you came for—sometimes you get what you need instead. What seemed like a straightforward skin issue required a comprehensive examination that opened doors I wasn't prepared to walk through.

A few days later, my phone rang with my doctor's number displayed. He informed me that I needed to start taking Vitamin D supplements immediately. Then came the news I wasn't expecting—my cholesterol levels were dangerously elevated.

He recommended cutting back significantly on sugar, butter, refined carbohydrates, and essentially all the ingredients that made food worth eating in my opinion. My heart sank as the implications became clear. The prescription might as well have read: "No more joy in your diet, effective immediately."

I had to confront the uncomfortable reality that I had been systematically damaging my body through my choices. I knew better. I knew exactly what maintaining health required. I had successfully implemented healthy habits before, then gradually abandoned them in favor of comfort and convenience.

I had stopped honestly assessing my reflection in the mirror. I had stopped weighing myself when the numbers became inconvenient. When clothes no longer fit comfortably, I simply purchased larger sizes and pretended nothing had changed. I was the queen of self-deception, ruling over a kingdom of stretchy pants and loose-fitting tops.

When Reality Gets Deadly Serious

I began seriously considering what these test results signified. Heart problems run extensively throughout my family tree. Further research revealed the sobering statistic that nearly half of Black women have high cholesterol—a silent killer that often shows no symptoms until serious damage occurs.

The gravity of my situation hit me with full force: What would happen to my children if I were no longer here? How would my husband navigate life without me? I still had so many plans, so many dreams, so much life I wanted to experience. My theoretical knowledge needed to align with practical action before it was too late. My profound love for my family ultimately outweighed my temporary affection for pancakes.

Fast-forward to early 2025, I finally decided to schedule another appointment I had been actively avoiding since turning 40—my first mammogram. In January, I booked both this screening and my yearly gynecological exam.

Fear had been mercilessly plaguing my mind throughout the latter part of 2024, whispering insidious suggestions that I was harboring illness within my body. I cannot adequately express how paralyzingly terrifying it is to face the unknown, the anxiety that accompanies health concerns creating a nearly unbearable burden.

After much prayer and reflection, I chose to confront these fears directly and schedule the necessary appointments, believing it far better to know and have a fighting chance than to remain ignorant or potentially ignore something requiring immediate attention. A particularly concerning symptom had been an annoying, persistent pain on the left side of my breast that frequently kept me awake during the night.

The Mammogram That Changed Everything

On the day of my mammogram, I asked my mother to accompany me for moral support. She graciously picked me up and walked alongside me into the imaging center. The procedure itself turned out to be surprisingly quick and far less uncomfortable than I had anticipated.

The technician casually mentioned that I might receive a callback for additional images, explaining that this was standard procedure for first-time mammograms, so I dismissed any potential concern. That casual dismissal lasted precisely until Saturday, when I received an official letter requesting my return for further imaging.

My heart immediately began racing while I simultaneously tried convincing myself that everything remained perfectly fine. I told my husband I would return the following Monday for these additional pictures, and then this anxiety-inducing chapter would conclude.

Until I called to schedule that follow-up appointment. The information the scheduling coordinator shared—details the technician had conveniently omitted—sent ice through my veins. They had identified something concerning ON THE LEFT SIDE OF MY BREAST! Yes, the exact location where I had been experiencing pain.

This wouldn't be a simple walk-in appointment; I needed to block out two full hours to meet with the radiologist for a comprehensive evaluation.

While processing this unsettling news, my annual physical results simultaneously arrived, indicating my "friend" high cholesterol had returned with a vengeance and I needed medication immediately. As if that weren't sufficient cause for concern, my lab work revealed abnormalities requiring further examination of my cervix to screen for CANCER!

This overwhelming flood of medical concerns crashed into my consciousness simultaneously. I had faced my fears by proactively seeking medical evaluation, and now reality had delivered a devastating counter-punch. The sobering truth became clear—I could maintain a slender physique yet still remain vulnerable to heart attacks or strokes without addressing my cholesterol levels properly.

Faith in the Face of Fear

I, again, requested time to attempt to manage my health naturally before starting pharmaceutical intervention. I scheduled the cervical biopsy and returned to the mammography clinic for additional imaging, this time bringing both my mother and daughter Genesis for extra support.

Throughout this challenging period, I had been diligently praying and fasting—my spiritual response when desperately needing divine breakthrough. Faith assured me that regardless of the outcome, I would ultimately be okay.

The technician displayed the concerning area on a monitor—speckled, paint-like marks and unusual vascular patterns. I heard virtually nothing of her technical explanation, my mind occupied with prayers and attempting to manage my escalating anxiety.

After enduring more "boob-smashing" images (a technical term I just invented), we waited nervously until being called back to consult with the radiologist. While walking back, someone nearby (who I'm convinced was dispatched by Satan himself) remarked loudly, "Oooh, that sounds serious." I refused to acknowledge the comment or make eye contact, continuing forward with my supportive family members.

The radiologist attempted explaining the images, using

analogies about teacups and discussing calcification patterns that barely registered in my anxious mind. Finally came the words I had been desperately hoping to hear: "They are benign and noncancerous. Return in a year for follow-up monitoring."

Praise erupted spontaneously from the depths of my soul—my greatest fears had not materialized into reality.

One major appointment successfully navigated, but I still faced the gynecologist for my cervical biopsy. Expecting something relatively routine similar to a standard Pap smear, I was woefully unprepared for the actual procedure.

Yes, there were the familiar stirrups and hospital gown, but the similarities ended there. The experience itself was memorably uncomfortable in ways I hadn't anticipated. Results wouldn't be available for another week—an interminable waiting period during which I strived to maintain positive thoughts and continue my prayers.

While entering a workshop for a High School afterschool program one Friday afternoon, my phone rang with the gynecology office number. The nurse delivered the news I had been praying for: no signs of cancer or abnormal cells detected. If "whew" were personified, it would have been me in that moment.

Your Turn to Choose Action Over Comfort

This brings me to you, my friend. Perhaps there's an area in your life where you clearly know what actions you should be taking. You've read the book, consulted with a coach, written detailed plans, created elaborate vision boards. Yet you haven't taken meaningful action toward what you know needs to be done.

Nobody can take these crucial steps for you. Your vision board, no matter how beautifully designed, remains merely a decorative item until you personally initiate movement toward those goals. If the comprehensive picture overwhelms you, break it down. Take it one step at a time. One pound at a time. One page at a time. One day at a time.

Whatever your particular challenge requires—do the thing consistently, and watch in amazement as what you truly desire begins gravitating toward you.

Sometimes life has to get uncomfortably real before we're willing to surrender our temporary comforts for lasting change. My story isn't about pancakes—it's about the stories we tell ourselves to avoid doing the hard thing, even when we know better. It's about choosing long-term health over momentary pleasure, choosing reality over delusion, and ultimately, choosing life over whatever comfort is holding us back.

What's your pancake? What comfort are you clinging to that's keeping you from the change you know you need? Whatever it is, I'm here to tell you that surrender isn't about giving up—it's about trading something good for something better. It's about letting go of what's comfortable to embrace what's possible.

And trust me, on the other side of that surrender is a life far sweeter than any pancake could ever be.

With love and a tiny bit of pancake batter still on my sleeve.

When Tears Don't Follow the Script

Can I let you in on something else, friends? I think I'm emotionally constipated.

If you're thinking, "Is this actually a thing?" Trust me, it is. And I'm living proof.

For example, I don't tend to cry at the conventionally appropriate moments. Anyone would reasonably expect that I would shed tears at the birth of a child or when receiving an extremely kind and unexpected gift. You'd probably anticipate witnessing genuine tears flowing when I read a heartfelt letter. Or when someone looks directly into my eyes while offering profound encouragement.

But me? No tears. Not one. Not even manufactured ones for the sake of social propriety.

I mean, most people DO cry in these situations, right? It seems like the natural, expected response. The movie script of life says "Insert tears here" at these moments, and everyone else seems to follow the stage directions perfectly.

I often find myself internally reaching for them because a tear or two would certainly help in certain situations. It would make others more comfortable, would align with the expected emotional script of the moment. I'll be standing there thinking, "Come on, tear ducts… DO SOMETHING.

Everyone's waiting!" But nope. Desert dry.

Instead, my waterworks arrive during entirely different circumstances – when things are just fine or when a random thought unexpectedly surfaces in my consciousness. Cue the unstoppable tears. No discernible pattern or explanation.

With me, you might encounter situations like: "Where were you when my mother-in-law surprised the kids with that elaborate backyard adventure set?" TEARS. Streaming, unstoppable tears.

"What happened at that completely ordinary board meeting last week?" TEARS. So many tears I had to fake an urgent phone call and rush off the Zoom.

Unusual, I know. Trust me, I surprise myself sometimes. The tears just flow unhindered, and I find myself thinking: "Really? Now? Do I absolutely have to cry at THIS precise moment? Do I have to cry in THIS particular place? Oh, come on!" It feels like my emotional wiring got crossed somewhere along the way, creating this unpredictable response system that rarely aligns with social expectations.

When the Tears Decided to Show Up Uninvited

It was 2019. Also my self-proclaimed year of YES (with gratitude to Shonda Rhimes for the inspiration). I had been selected to participate in a prestigious leadership development fellowship program, which, by the way, I was SUPER excited about.

On the first day, I and nineteen other fellows were assigned this somewhat childish exercise where we each created a visual roadmap of our lives. I approached mine with relative ease and minimal emotional investment. I've always enjoyed drawing, so this seemed straightforward enough. No big deal, right?

Just another ice-breaker activity.

After completing our individual maps, we were instructed to share our drawings and guide the group through our life's journey. One by one, my fellow participants stepped forward. I observed as each of them invariably became emotional, tears welling up as they recounted particularly significant or challenging moments in their lives.

"Emotional saps," I thought to myself with a mixture of judgment and perhaps a hint of envy. "Pfhuh." (That's the sound of me mentally rolling my eyes, in case you're wondering.)

Then came my turn. I stood before the group and began methodically walking them through my life's journey. No tears. Not one droplet. My eyes remained perfectly dry as I recounted childhood experiences, educational milestones, career transitions – until I began discussing my children.

What happened next can only be described as being overcome with what church-goers might call "church giggles," except with tears instead of laughter. It was an unexpected eruption of emotion. I cried so copiously that articulating words became nearly impossible.

Y'all, I'm not talking about a delicate, dignified single tear rolling gracefully down my cheek. I'm talking about the ugly cry. The kind with shoulder-shaking sobs and incoherent mumbling and—worst of all—snot. So. Much. Snot.

The experience was profoundly disarming. I felt as if I stood completely exposed before them, stripped of my carefully constructed composure, allowing them to glimpse something raw and unfiltered. A wave of embarrassment washed over me as I awkwardly wiped away evidence of my emotional outburst from my nose.

I genuinely look forward to asking God someday why human crying must involve nasal secretions. Tremendously undignified. Was that really necessary in the design? Couldn't tears just come from our eyes and leave our noses out of it? But I digress.

The Emotional Rulebook I Never Got

When I permit myself to reflect more deeply on this pattern, I arrive at the conclusion that somewhere in my psychological development, I formed an association between crying and vulnerability, or perhaps even weakness. You know the old saying: "Big girls don't cry."

I intellectually understand this isn't accurate, and I'm actively working to recalibrate this thinking. I'm basically trying to rewrite my emotional rulebook, but apparently my tear ducts didn't get the memo.

Let me be absolutely clear on this point: Crying is entirely acceptable. Understood?

Additionally, NOT crying is equally acceptable. Understood?

So why am I sharing all this with you?

The thing about tears is they function somewhat like an emotional cleansing. The only exception I'll note here involves those individuals who possess the uncanny ability to cry on command and strategically deploy this skill to manipulate situations and people. My daughter Rhema has that gift. I'm not referring to those tears. Those can be reserved for "another conversation entirely." (And if you have this superpower, please use it responsibly.)

I'm talking about authentic tears. The ones that emerge reluctantly, the ones that leave us feeling uncomfortably vulnerable, the ones that have been suppressed and contained for extended periods – those are the tears that often reveal fundamental truths about ourselves.

What Authenticity Actually Looks Like

Authenticity. Simply that. Being exactly who you are, standing in your own unique *you-ness*.

Webster's dictionary defines it as "not counterfeit or copied." Sounds simple enough, right? But we all know it's anything but simple in real life.

Here's my personal definition: Authenticity is the state of being that fully embodies one's complete self without apology. It also means embracing every element of your identity and presenting yourself exactly as you are, without filters or modifications to meet others' expectations. The realness.

I can't control how I cry at these unexpected, seemingly inappropriate moments, but this unpredictable emotional response pattern represents perhaps the most practical illustration I can offer about authenticity. My tears emerge exactly as they are – unscripted, unfiltered, and often inconveniently timed. Kind of like life itself.

In all seriousness, authenticity manifests in my acceptance that I generally dislike crying publicly – that's simply part of who I am. No pretense. I don't cry when social conventions suggest I should. I've abandoned attempts to produce tears to impress or satisfy observers.

I've released the pressure to conform to "normal" emotional expression patterns, particularly regarding crying. This exemplifies authentic living.

And you might wonder why this matters so significantly?

Because profound freedom exists in authenticity. You don't

have to make up reactions or conceal your true responses. You simply experience the freedom to exist naturally because that's who you inherently are. No masks or performative behaviors.

It resembles how I felt during that unexpected emotional release before my fellow program participants – vulnerable yet strangely liberated. Like I'd been holding my breath for years and finally exhaled.

The Freedom and Fear of Being Real

Ironically, while authenticity offers tremendous freedom, it simultaneously introduces fear. Fear of not fulfilling others' expectations upon realizing certain expected behaviors don't align with your genuine self (perhaps they never did).

That's the inevitable cost of authentic living. It can be terrifying to stand apart. To be the exception. Sometimes it creates profound isolation. Particularly when observing countless individuals seemingly pursuing identical paths toward popularity, recognition, and approval.

It's unnerving… it's deeply frightening to diverge from established norms. It's terrifying to present yourself without embellishment or strategic editing.

But it's authentic. It's genuine. It's authentic to be simply, wholly you. (And yes, I notice that rhymed. Sometimes I accidentally write greeting card slogans. It's my superpower.)

Perhaps you're wondering how someone can truly embody authenticity if they remain uncertain about their core identity. There exists a particular beauty in acknowledging that uncertainty and embracing the freedom to discover yourself gradually.

The experience of comfort in your authentic identity, rather than one borrowed or even appropriated from others, offers a deeper richness. Dedicate time to self-discovery. Because continuously adjusting yourself to fit a predetermined mold not designed for you eventually becomes exhaustingly unsustainable.

Trust me on this. It's like trying to wear shoes three sizes too small. You might squeeze into them for a special occasion, but try walking around in them day after day? Your feet will revolt. Your soul works the same way.

When the World Tries to Rewrite Your Story

I've had to confront this reality repeatedly throughout my life. Like many women, particularly women of color, I've received countless explicit and implicit messages about who I should be, how I should express myself, when I should speak up, and when I should remain silent.

I've been told my natural hair wasn't "professional enough," my voice was "too assertive," my emotions "too visible" or conversely "not visible enough." Each message suggested that my authentic self wasn't acceptable, that I needed modification to fit some external standard of worthiness.

For years, I attempted these adjustments. I straightened my hair for important meetings. I modulated my voice to sound "less threatening." I practiced appropriate emotional responses for various situations.

The result? Exhaustion. Bone-deep weariness from maintaining these various performances. And worse – disconnection from myself. I began losing touch with my genuine reactions, preferences, and expressions because I'd spent so long suppressing them.

It was like I'd created this perfect character for the world to interact with, but somewhere along the way, I forgot it wasn't actually me. I was just the exhausted actress behind the mask, desperately trying to remember all my lines.

The World Needs Your Unique Brand of Weird

Trust me when I say the world eagerly awaits the authentic you. Why? Because you represent a unique gift specifically prepared for this universe. Your particular combination of strengths, weaknesses, perspectives, experiences, and expressions exists nowhere else. When you withhold your authenticity, you deprive others of that singular gift.

I've seen this truth manifested repeatedly through my work with young women. When I create safe spaces for them to appear genuinely, without pretense or performance, the transformation is remarkable. Their ideas become more innovative, their connections more meaningful, their contributions more impactful. Not because they've improved themselves, but because they've allowed their true selves to emerge without apology.

This doesn't mean authenticity always feels comfortable. Some days, being genuinely yourself feels like wearing shoes on the wrong feet – technically possible but awkward and uncomfortable. You might question whether you've miscalculated, whether returning to familiar performances might be simpler.

In those moments, I encourage gentle persistence. Authenticity is a muscle that strengthens with use. The discomfort you feel isn't a sign you're doing it wrong – it's evidence that you're growing beyond old limitations.

Think about it like this: if you've spent years sitting in a tiny box, standing up to your full height is going to feel strange at first. Your muscles will protest. You might wobble a bit. That doesn't mean you should climb back into the box – it means your body is adjusting to the freedom of standing tall.

Your Permission Slip to Be Real

Consider the people you most admire, those whose presence feels like a gift. I suspect what draws you to them isn't perfection but authenticity – their willingness to be genuinely themselves, complete with flaws, quirks, and unexpected responses. They've given you permission, through their example, to bring your whole self forward too.

So whether you cry at unexpected moments like me, or you never cry at all, whether your laugh is too loud by conventional standards or your opinions too strong, whether your appearance challenges norms or your interests defy stereotypes – bring it all. Bring your whole, unedited self.

I'm not promising it will always be easy. There will be people who prefer the performance, who find comfort in the familiar scripts and get uncomfortable when you deviate from them. There will be situations where authenticity comes with costs. There will be moments of doubt when you wonder if the old masks might be easier.

But I can promise you this: the freedom of authentic living is worth the discomfort. The connections you'll form when people respond to the real you are infinitely more nourishing than any validation of your performance could ever be.

And here's another truth I've discovered: authenticity is contagious. When you give yourself permission to be real, you create ripples that extend far beyond yourself. You silently grant others the same freedom. Your courage becomes a gift that keeps giving.

So the next time I find myself crying at some completely

random and socially inappropriate moment, I'm going to try to embrace it as a reminder that my emotions don't follow anyone else's script – and that's perfectly okay. I'm going to let those tears fall without apology, messy and inconvenient as they may be.

Because being authentic isn't about being perfect. It's about being perfectly, wonderfully, uniquely you.

Just be!

Learning Life's Lessons the Long Way Around

When I was young, my mom used to punish us differently than my dad. There was a sharp contrast in their approaches that taught me early about different communication styles.

My dad was a disciplinarian of few words. He would just punish us and get it over with - very practical and straight to the point, like you would probably expect from a traditional father figure. Three pops on the butt, tears, a lesson about why what you did was wrong, and then we moved on. Efficient, predictable, and ultimately forgettable in the grand scheme of childhood memories.

Not my mom. Oh honey, she was operating on a whole different system.

She wasn't particularly skilled at corporal punishment anyway. She was every inch a woman who understood that physical force wasn't her strongest asset. She couldn't bring herself to exert the energy needed for an effective spanking, you know? I suspect she also knew deep down that her real power lay elsewhere.

So even when she did attempt to spank us, it was nothing compared to what my dad would ordinarily deliver. Or anyone else for that matter. The gentleness of her hand made me perform more than actually suffer. I would dramatically act like I was in excruciating pain rather than actually experiencing any real discomfort. But I maintained the performance so the ordeal wouldn't drag on longer than necessary.

"Owww, Mama! Please stop! I'll never do it again!" I'd wail, while thinking about what snack I might have when this little charade concluded. Academy Award-worthy stuff, let me tell you.

The Great Padding Incident

I vividly remember one particular incident when my mother promised me a spanking, and I had conjured up in my mind that she was finally going to deliver the worst punishment I'd ever experienced. My imagination ran wild with fearsome scenarios. The offense was truly outrageous – though for the life of me I can't recall exactly what it was now – and I was absolutely certain that I had aggravated her enough for her to tap deeply into some hidden reservoir of disciplinary energy, enough to actually give me the spanking of my life.

It was the suspense of waiting for her to return home that nearly undid me. Every minute felt like an hour as I anticipated her arrival. For reasons I couldn't articulate, I just couldn't predict what to expect. The uncertainty was worse than any punishment.

Adding to my anxiety, my older sister also believed mom was going to exceed her usual spanking capabilities this time. "You've really done it now," she said, shaking her head with that particular sibling satisfaction of seeing another in trouble. "Mom is gonna let you HAVE it." (Isn't it amazing how siblings can simultaneously be your best friend and worst enemy in the span of five minutes?)

So, in a moment of what we thought was genius, my sister and I decided it would be strategic for me to pad my pants to soften the anticipated blows of my mother's hand. We weren't expecting her usual half-hearted taps – no, we anticipated genuine, forceful blows that would require protection.

With solemn determination, we began to stuff everything we could find from our underwear drawer into my pants. Panties, stockings, even a small towel found their way into the makeshift padding. I essentially had a Brazilian butt lift before it was even a cosmetic procedure people paid thousands for. Looking back, I must have looked utterly ridiculous with my disproportionately enhanced posterior.

Somehow, in our juvenile reasoning, we thought this elaborate deception would actually work. What were we even thinking? I mean, how could we have allowed ourselves to entertain even the slightest notion that my mom wouldn't notice my suddenly enormous backside?

Oh no! Perhaps we expected her to simply overlook this dramatic anatomical change and just proceed with the punishment as though nothing was unusual. "Yes, my daughter always had the bottom half of a Kardashian. Nothing to see here!"

Long story short, when my mother finally arrived home and called me in for the reckoning, she immediately noticed something was amiss. As I waddled into her room, trying to maintain a normal gait despite the extensive padding, her expression shifted from stern to bewildered.

When she realized what I had done – as panties and stockings began shifting and peeking out from my waistband – she couldn't bring herself to continue with the spanking. How could she? The entire situation had become utterly ridiculous.

She simply stared at me, shook her head slowly, and went into her bedroom without another word about the incident. She never mentioned it again.

Now that I'm a mother myself, I understand with absolute certainty that she retreated to her room to release the laughter she couldn't contain in my presence. I can picture her now, face buried in a pillow, shoulders shaking with silent mirth at her daughter's absurd attempt at self-preservation. I would've done exactly the same thing if my kids pulled a stunt like that!

The Power of a Mother's Words

What my mother didn't realize then – or perhaps she knew exactly what she was doing – was that while spanking wasn't her particular talent, talking most certainly was. And still is to this day.

Let me offer you this piece of wisdom: don't ever get in trouble with my mom. She will talk to you with such persistence, such eloquence, such emotional depth that you might find yourself confessing to something you didn't even do, just to make the verbal deluge stop.

And almost invariably, these epic conversations would end with either her crying or you crying. Sometimes both, in a strange emotional duet that left everyone exhausted. The CIA could learn a thing or two from my mother's interrogation techniques, I'm just saying.

My mother is unquestionably one of the most powerful speakers I've ever encountered. Her words are compelling, her delivery animated, her vocabulary precise and impactful. Her discussions aren't merely conversations – they're soul-searching expeditions, or more accurately, probing examinations of your conscience.

It's almost as though she possesses some supernatural ability to read your mind, knowing exactly which psychological buttons to push with her carefully selected words. She instinctively understands which topics to avoid because she recognizes they might provoke defensiveness rather than reflection.

She somehow manages to captivate and maintain your complete attention while she speaks. And when she decides to emphasize a point – Lord have mercy – she goes IN on it with such intensity that you can't help but absorb her message.

I suppose this natural talent explains why she eventually became a preacher. She performs this verbal magic effortlessly, without breaking a sweat. Just a strategic tear here and there, especially when she wants to persuade you to do something you'd ordinarily resist. Those tears – so powerful, so effective, and as I now suspect, sometimes so deliberately deployed.

You know how some people have a signature dance move or a catchphrase? Well, my mother has a signature verbal transition. Whenever she senses she's approaching the conclusion of one of these marathon talks, she employs her distinctive phrase: "I said all that to say…"

The first time I became conscious of this linguistic pattern, I remember thinking, "Wait, what? So all of those other statements before were just preliminary to this one thing you're only now about to say? Are you suggesting this final point is more important than everything else you've spent the last forty-five minutes discussing? Are you implying that all those other words couldn't stand independently meaningful? They were merely pointing to this single culminating idea?"

Good Lord! The verbal journey seemed so unnecessarily

expansive. It was like driving from New York to Boston by way of Florida.

The Legacy of Long-Winded Love

That phrase – "I said all that to say" – has stayed with me throughout my life, particularly as I write this book. I recognize now that I've inherited a narrative style remarkably similar to my mother's.

We long-winded communicators can discover the story within the story, uncovering layers of meaning that might not be immediately apparent. One observation can lead us down an unexpected path we hadn't originally intended to explore.

Sometimes, if we're not mindful of our tendency to verbally meander, a single tangential point can make us temporarily forget what we initially intended to say. When that happens, we must find another theme that can somehow encompass all the detours we've taken, bringing coherence to what might otherwise seem like verbal wandering.

Have you ever started telling a story and halfway through realized you've gone so far off track that you've forgotten your original point? Then you have to quickly come up with a new, meaningful conclusion that somehow ties everything together? That's basically the story of my life. And apparently, it's genetic.

This chapter stands as an appreciative tribute to my mom or, as I affectionately call her, mama. Because if it weren't for those long, sometimes dreadful talks and impromptu sermons throughout my childhood, I wouldn't have developed my current appreciation for the journey a message can take.

Without that foundation, I probably wouldn't understand

that even in life, we take detours but eventually arrive somewhere meaningful. In both storytelling and living, the path rarely follows a straight line.

The profound truth I've come to understand is that you often discover why you needed to experience all those detours once you reach your destination. Most times, anyway.

You can begin in one place, take an unexpected diversion down memory lane, pause to reflect, perhaps shed a tear, momentarily forget your original topic, and then somehow find your way back to the core message for a satisfying conclusion. Life works that way too – we rarely appreciate the detours until they lead us to unexpected blessings.

In fact, those seemingly long-winded stories often make the main point more accessible and relatable. They provide context, emotional resonance, and memorable illustrations that help anchor abstract concepts in concrete reality. I genuinely believe my own stories serve the same purpose – if I may say so myself. They're not merely entertaining diversions; they're essential elements that make the message more digestible and meaningful.

I Said All That to Say…

I said all that to say, there is a meaningful message embedded within every story if you approach it with patience and attentiveness. Every story has some essential truth, waiting to be discovered by the discerning listener or reader.

Like the parables Jesus used to teach complex spiritual principles, stories often can simplify difficult truths, making them more accessible and personally relevant. They bring abstract concepts home to you in ways that direct statements sometimes cannot.

The best stories resonate because they bear some resemblance or connection to your own experiences, creating bridges of understanding and empathy.

I said all that to say, allow yourself to fully absorb the stories you encounter throughout life – including those in this book – and follow the occasional diversions with patience and openness. There's a message waiting for you somewhere within those narrative journeys, a message that will likely resonate with your particular circumstances because, in some mystical way, it was tailor-made precisely for you.

Just as my mother's winding tales somehow always managed to address exactly what I needed to hear, even when I wasn't aware of needing it.

You know what's funny? As much as I used to dread those long talks as a child, I find myself using the exact same techniques with my own children now. The other day, I caught myself mid-lecture and realized I had been talking for twenty minutes straight, complete with dramatic pauses, rhetorical questions, and even a strategic tear. The apple didn't just fall close to the tree; it's basically still attached to the branch.

So if you ever find yourself in a conversation with me that seems to be taking the scenic route, now you know who to blame. I'm just my mother's daughter, finding my way to the point through winding paths and unexpected detours. And somehow, when we finally get there, the journey makes the destination all the more meaningful.

I said all that to say… thank you, Mama, for teaching me that the longest path to a truth is often the one that sticks with us the longest.

Green Isn't Always Ugly

During the pandemic era, there was a new social app I'd been spending way too much time on. Like, "Should I be concerned about myself?" levels of time. That app, while I am sure still exists has lost its allure much like Myspace or…I'm gonna say it…Black Planet (although I hear Black Planet is making a comeback). Anyway, what I found absolutely fascinating about this platform is that it basically lets you eavesdrop on conversations about literally anything under the sun. There are even rooms where people just sit together in digital silence, which is honestly kind of weirdly beautiful in our hyperconnected, notification-obsessed world.

One afternoon, my phone lit up with an invitation to join one of these rooms. I'm not gonna lie—I felt a little nervous about hitting that "join" button. Why? Because I'd previously made the rookie mistake of entering a similar room and suddenly found myself yanked up to an invisible stage to speak. No warning. No preparation. Just BAM—spotlight on me! Cue the social anxiety sweats, the racing heart, and me frantically hitting the exit button faster than you can say "introvert nightmare."

This time, though, I gave myself a little pep talk. "Come on, girl. You can do this. Just join as a listener. Nobody's forcing you to speak." So I took a deep breath and entered the digital room, clutching my invisible security blanket.

To my delight, I discovered a group of female entrepreneurs having this incredibly thoughtful conversation about women and the scarcity mindset. The dialogue immediately hooked me—you know that feeling when you're nodding along so hard you might give yourself whiplash? That was me. I found myself mentally forming responses, thinking, "Ooh, I have something to add to that!" and "Yes, girl, preach!"

And then, the unthinkable happened.

I WAS INVITED TO THE STAGE!

My fight-or-flight response kicked in like a caffeinated kangaroo, but this time I mentally sat it down for a chat. "Not today, anxiety. We're staying." I accepted the invitation and joined these accomplished women in their conversation. After hearing several of them share their experiences with such beautiful honesty, suddenly it was my turn to speak.

Finding My Voice (And Using It)

Having recently completed Julia Cameron's twelve-week program in "The Artist's Way" (which, by the way, should be required reading for every human with a pulse), I felt newly liberated to talk about things that used to make me squirm. I no longer felt like I needed to pretend I had it all figured out. The thought of sharing my authentic thoughts on this topic felt surprisingly natural. Plus, I was among women who seemed to "get it," which created this cozy little bubble of psychological safety.

So I shared my perspective on what I believe is often at the root of the scarcity mindset—the "j word." Jealousy. Yep, I said it. The big, green, uncomfortable emotion that nobody wants to admit to.

I openly confessed that I sometimes experience jealousy. I emphasized that acknowledging and naming these feelings is something women should practice more often. After sharing some additional thoughts, I handed the virtual microphone back to the hosts, feeling pretty good about my contribution.

The next woman who spoke began with: "Well, I can't say that I've ever had a problem with jealousy, but I can totally agree with…"

I've inserted those little dots after "with" because my brain literally short-circuited at that point. I processed absolutely nothing beyond those first twelve words. From that moment, I spiraled through more emotions than a teenager watching an episode of Outer Banks.

The Emotional Roller coaster Begins

Initially, I felt that familiar sinking feeling—you know the one. That "I just shared something super vulnerable and got completely shut down" embarrassment. Had I just publicly admitted to a group of strangers that I've struggled with jealousy, only to have the next speaker casually dismiss it as a non-issue because she claimed never to have experienced it herself?

Do you understand how threatening this felt to my self-perception? Not necessarily in the eyes of these strangers, but in my own estimation? It was like showing up to a potluck with my grandma's secret recipe that I'd spent hours making, only to have someone glance at it and say, "Oh, I never eat *that* kind of food."

Those feelings quickly morphed into skepticism. Come ON now. Is there actually a human being walking this planet who has never, not once, experienced jealousy? Even if we accept the possibility that she's completely overcome jealousy (which, good for her!), is it realistic to claim NEVER having experienced it? Not even when she was five years old and someone else got the toy she wanted? Not even in high school when her crush asked someone else to prom? Not EVER?

I know judging others isn't exactly aligned with my values, but in that moment, I found myself doing it anyway. Perhaps I should throw these reactions out the window and simply acknowledge that this woman likely hasn't embarked on the same journey of uncomfortable self-reflection that I've been stumbling through.

I won't sugarcoat it—her comment stuck with me for days afterward. It seemed almost ridiculous that I started questioning my own progress and feeling somewhat ashamed for acknowledging my ongoing work navigating the ebbs and flows of jealousy. It almost felt like all the personal development work I had invested in building my self-awareness had been invalidated in a few casual seconds.

This wasn't the woman's fault, of course. Her comment just shined a spotlight on an area of my life that clearly needed some additional attention.

What My Jealousy Actually Looks Like

Let's get something straight—jealous feelings pop up at various unexpected times for me. This doesn't mean I transform into some green-tinged mythological monster, stomping around and roaring at everyone experiencing success. (Although, not gonna lie, that mental image is kind of hilarious.)

No, my experience of jealousy manifests more internally.

For me, jealousy typically signals something I desire but haven't yet obtained, or something I'm actively working toward but haven't yet achieved.

It surfaces when I'm mindlessly scrolling through social media and come across a friend's celebratory post. And let me be crystal clear—I am genuinely happy for my friends! It's just that sometimes, alongside that genuine happiness, there's a little pang of jealousy about their successes.

Maybe she landed the dream job she's always wanted, or someone else is posting selfies with Oprah Winfrey (and everyone in my circle knows meeting Oprah is basically my version of climbing Mount Everest). That "why-not-me" feeling gradually sets up shop in my mind, making itself uncomfortably at home until it becomes nearly unbearable.

When I notice these feelings becoming too intrusive, I typically shut off my device or find something else to do. After all, who actively seeks out the distinctive sting of jealousy? It's like intentionally putting on shoes that are two sizes too small and then going for a long walk. No thank you!

The Roots of My Green-Eyed Monster

I used to believe jealousy was something shameful or a sign of emotional immaturity. In certain cases, it absolutely is. For these reasons, I would push down those inevitable jealous feelings because I didn't want to be like Cain from the Bible. You probably remember him—the guy who killed his brother because God favored his brother's sacrifice? Okay, so I feel like I need to explain this a little better so people who actually read their Bible won't be all judgy. Abel brought God the very best and first while Cain simply brought an offering. Doesn't seem like much but if you check out any portion of the Old

Testament, God wasn't playing around when it came to doing things with excellence. Anyway, I digress.

There's certainly more complexity to that story, but I'm not trying to deliver a Sunday School lesson here. Considering my upbringing, I mention this simply to show where my perspective came from.

In my childhood home, practically every life situation corresponded to a biblical story or verse that my parents could quote with perfect timing, effectively ending any argument. These scriptural references emerged like well-played cards in a strategic game. And remarkably, this approach always worked—because honestly, who wants to disappoint Jesus?

During my younger years, I experienced intense jealousy toward my older sister. There was no logical reason for these feelings. I simply wanted to outperform her in everything. I wanted to be my parents' favorite child. Looking back, I recognize that I behaved like an entitled little brat who couldn't stand sharing the spotlight. And if you're guessing, yes, I AM A MIDDLE CHILD.

Making matters worse, my talented sister wrote an original play for our church called "Do You Have The Time." It was objectively impressive, though I would have rather eaten a live cockroach than admit that at the time.

To my absolute horror and indignation, I wasn't given a lead role in the production. In fact, I wasn't included in the cast AT ALL. The injustice! How could she exclude me? Adding insult to injury, she cast my boyfriend in the play—yes, the very production from which I had been completely omitted. Oh, the AUDACITY!

He played the leading male role, with another young woman as his romantic interest. They needed to rehearse their scenes together, and I found myself consumed with jealousy. I'm still not sure which was worse: my jealousy toward my sister for creating a successful play, or my jealousy regarding my boyfriend and his stage partner.

Needless to say, I did a terrible job pretending these circumstances didn't affect me emotionally. On opening night, I maintained a forced smile through barely contained tears, finding it nearly unbearable to watch my boyfriend pretend to be married to someone else, even in a fictional context.

I experienced what can only be described as an epic emotional meltdown.

That situation perfectly exemplifies immature jealousy—a profoundly irrational emotional response. It's amazing how trying to hide, suppress, or avoid issues that need direct confrontation often just makes them worse. I doubt I had the emotional capacity to fully express or acknowledge my jealousy as a teenager. But as an adult with greater perspective, I can look back at my younger self and recognize that I behaved like an irrational, jealous adolescent. (Shocking, I know—a teenager acting like a teenager!)

The Silent Green Epidemic

These are exactly the kinds of situations people typically avoid discussing openly. Who willingly admits to seeing a friend's social media announcement about completing their Master's degree and deliberately not engaging with it because they're feeling "a little jelly" (jealousy)? No one.

It's considerably easier to claim not having seen the post. Or use that universally accepted excuse: "I'm not particularly active on social media"—when, in reality, we all know the truth. We've been on there for three hours straight, liking cat videos and taking quizzes to find out which sandwich best represents our personality.

In retrospect, perhaps my fellow participant in that virtual room genuinely belongs to that rare category of individuals who have never experienced jealousy. Alternatively, she may not have reached a point where she's prepared to confront her personal truth.

What I know with absolute certainty is that authentic self-knowledge eventually finds you, regardless of how effectively you try to avoid it.

Turning Green into Gold

Full disclosure: I haven't been "cured" of jealousy. Don't let anyone (including yourself) create false expectations, because there's no magical solution for instantly resolving difficult emotions. There's no prescription medication for it. No comprehensive ten-step program guaranteeing complete elimination of jealousy.

Even if such a solution existed, I'm not convinced I would pursue it. Why? Because I've learned to use jealousy constructively now. Does that statement seem strange? It shouldn't. Jealousy serves a purpose in my personal development.

And here's how this transformation occurred...

Jealousy now functions as an indicator highlighting areas requiring potential growth. When I observe someone else's success and notice feelings of discomfort arising, I recognize this may signal that I haven't yet invested enough effort to experience my own success in that area.

In these moments, I tell myself: "Girl, you need to recommit to your goals and take decisive action!" It's like having a built-in GPS that recalculates when I've veered off course from where I genuinely want to be.

Alternatively, it might indicate I'm simply experiencing an emotional overreaction and need to inventory my blessings and accomplishments to regain perspective. When this happens, I follow through accordingly. I sit down with my journal and write out everything I'm grateful for, everything I've accomplished, and all the ways I've grown. It's like hitting the reset button on my emotional computer.

Beyond identifying areas for growth, jealousy often reveals our authentic desires. Sometimes we dismiss or minimize our true ambitions, trying to convince ourselves we don't really want certain achievements or experiences. When jealousy emerges unexpectedly, it often unveils what we genuinely desire but haven't fully acknowledged.

It's like when I insisted for years that I didn't care about having a book published, but then felt that distinctive jealous twinge every time a friend announced their book deal. My jealousy was basically calling out my own self-deception, saying, "Um, excuse me? We both know you're lying to yourself right now."

Additionally, I've discovered that properly channeled jealousy can become motivational fuel. Rather than allowing it to manifest as resentment toward others' success, I transform it into inspiration. If someone else achieved something remarkable, their success demonstrates possibility.

Their accomplishment proves that my goal isn't impossible—someone has already traversed that path. This perspective converts jealousy from a destructive force into creative energy. It's like turning compost into garden soil—the same material that could just sit there stinking can actually help new things grow!

I've also found immense freedom in openly acknowledging jealous feelings, rather than pretending they don't exist. The energy previously devoted to suppressing or disguising these emotions becomes available for more constructive purposes.

There's something remarkably liberating about simply saying, "I feel jealous about that achievement, and that's okay. Now, what can I learn from this feeling?" It's like finally putting down a heavy backpack you've been carrying for miles—the immediate relief is palpable.

The Jealousy Journey

This evolution in my relationship with jealousy didn't happen overnight. It required extensive self-reflection, numerous uncomfortable conversations with myself, and consistent practice in reframing negative emotions as information rather than character flaws.

I still experience jealousy—I doubt that will ever change completely—but my response to that emotion has transformed dramatically. It's like the difference between being caught in a sudden downpour without an umbrella versus dancing in the rain because you came prepared.

By acknowledging jealousy rather than denying it, I've discovered one of life's interesting paradoxes: the emotions we most actively resist often hold the greatest potential for personal growth. When we bring our shadows into the light, examining them with compassion rather than judgment, they lose their power over us and may even reveal unexpected gifts.

Think about it: How many times have you denied feeling jealous even to yourself? How much energy have you spent avoiding or suppressing those feelings? What might happen if you simply said, "Yep, I'm feeling jealous right now," and then got curious about what that jealousy is trying to tell you?

So the next time you feel that familiar twinge when scrolling through social media or watching someone else receive the recognition you crave, consider leaning all the way into it. Instead, welcome it as a messenger bearing potentially valuable information about your desires, your progress, and perhaps even your next steps toward personal fulfillment.

Jealousy doesn't have to be the villain in your story. With a little reframing and a lot of self-compassion, it might just become an unexpected bestie in your quest toward becoming the realest version of yourself.

And if someone ever claims they've never experienced jealousy? Well, you can smile knowingly and silently congratulate yourself on having the courage to acknowledge your full spectrum of emotions—even the green ones.

Fear is Not a Stop Sign

I guess you can call me a scared cat. Actually, no "guessing" needed—I'm officially claiming the title. That characterization has been remarkably consistent throughout my life. I'm never the one running toward conflict or danger. Never. That's an absolute certainty. My typical response involves running first and asking clarifying questions only after I've reached a safe distance—preferably from another zip code.

So, what precisely was I afraid of?

Oh honey, what wasn't I afraid of?

I was afraid of the dark—that mysterious absence of light where my imagination worked overtime, turning every shadow into a potential serial killer or monster under the bed.

I was afraid of loud noises—those sudden, jarring sounds that make your heart leap into your throat without warning. Fire alarms? Forget it. Balloons popping? Instant tears.

I was afraid of ghosts—those ethereal entities my young mind couldn't comprehend but absolutely believed existed. Probably waiting in my closet. Definitely hiding in the basement or under the bed and some of y'all don't let your limbs dangle over the bed for that VERY reason (don't judge me).

I was afraid of pretty much anything you could possibly name. Spiders? Definitely. Heights? Absolutely. Public speaking? Without question. Rejection? With every fiber of my being.

If there was a Fear Olympics, I'd be taking home gold in multiple categories. I was basically a professional at being afraid.

When the Storm Came Calling

I vividly remember an incident from my childhood. My family and I traveled to Louisiana for a church conference, a trip that seemed exciting until nature decided to show off and remind us who's really boss.

One night at the hotel, a formidable storm descended upon us. The rain pounded against the windows while the wind howled with such ferocity that it seemed determined to tear the building apart. In my small, impressionable mind, I became absolutely convinced the hotel roof would be violently ripped away by the merciless gusts.

I simply couldn't comprehend how my parents and siblings appeared so remarkably unconcerned. How could they maintain such calm? Didn't they feel the very foundation shaking beneath us? Was I somehow the only one noticing the boisterous intensity of the wind?

And the thunder—it crashed with such volume and authority that I genuinely believed Jesus himself was descending to collect us all. Like, "That's it, folks! The rapture is happening NOW, in this Holiday Inn in New Orleans!"

My perceptive mother noticed the inner turmoil my little soul was experiencing. She gently suggested I pray if I felt afraid. Instead, I retreated to a corner and began singing—not praying, but singing. Because that's the intuitive response when facing imminent doom, right?

Like the musicians on the sinking Titanic, I attempted to cope through melody. Eventually, I resorted to covering my head with a pillow, creating a makeshift sanctuary until the storm finally subsided. The relief I felt was profound. Whew!

When you're small, storms impact you differently. The sheer scale of things beyond your control becomes overwhelmingly apparent, and feelings of helplessness wash over you like the rain itself.

While I've outgrown my fear of meteorological events (mostly), I still navigate through metaphorical storms that transport me back to that powerless child I once was in New Orleans. That particular variety of fear proves truly paralyzing, systematically robbing you of joy and preventing forward movement. It's like emotional quicksand—the more you struggle against it, the deeper you sink.

When Fear Hits Home

The first time I witnessed a Grand Mal seizure, I was a married woman with children of my own. This particular storm chose my daughter as its target. She was nine years old—still just a child herself.

It happened on what had begun as an ordinary Saturday. She had been experiencing persistent headaches that resisted relief. Her behavior had become increasingly atypical, and she progressively lost awareness of fundamental things like the location of the bathroom or how to navigate back to her bedroom.

The fear that gripped me was absolute. At one point, I anticipated she might vomit, but instead, she began shaking uncontrollably. I was utterly horrified. I found myself completely unprepared, without any instinctive knowledge of appropriate action. I became paralyzed and helpless.

This time, I didn't hide in a corner singing, but I experienced no less terror. What I discovered, though, is that sometimes you can perform courageous acts despite overwhelming fear, especially when the well-being of someone you love hangs in the balance.

That terrifying experience initiated a prolonged journey that fundamentally transformed my life. Countless times I felt the desperate urge to flee from the hospital or simply drive without destination or purpose. But I recognized my daughter needed me to remain present and advocate for her, even when fear threatened to overtake me. So, I confronted fear, perhaps for the first time in my life.

And yet, fear doesn't conveniently stop after a single confrontation. Fear doesn't check its calendar and say, "Well, I've had my time with her. Let me move on to someone else now."

The Entrepreneur's Anxiety Package Deal

When contemplating leaving my secure corporate position to launch my own business, fear emerged again, wearing a different mask. I found myself preoccupied with all the potential judgments people might express if they discovered I was actively pursuing entrepreneurial dreams while simultaneously caring for a medically fragile child.

The unspoken assumption: if I possessed sufficient capacity to start a business, why couldn't I simply return to traditional employment? No one actually verbalized these criticisms, but the accuser residing in my mind repeatedly did so with remarkable cruelty and persistence.

My inner critic had apparently attended law school and was now working pro bono, building cases against me 24/7. She was relentless, gathering evidence from every corner of my life, presenting arguments that would make Supreme Court justices tremble.

And still, fear doesn't relent. It doesn't call a timeout or take a vacation. Fear is that unwanted houseguest who keeps extending their stay, rearranging your furniture, and eating all your favorite snacks.

When the World Turned Upside Down

The COVID-19 pandemic introduced an entirely new dimension of fear. The concept seemed surreal initially—could I genuinely contract an illness severe enough to cause death from a virus spreading indiscriminately across the globe? Surely not!

I became terrified of venturing outside our home. As if that weren't sufficiently challenging, I subsequently experienced anxiety attacks from the prolonged confinement within our house. How was I expected to endure indefinite isolation for a duration no authority could definitively predict?

And relentlessly, fear continues its pursuit. Fear is nothing if not persistent. Like that one determined mosquito in your bedroom that somehow evades every swat and returns to buzz in your ear just as you're falling asleep.

When the World Outside Feels Dangerous

The racial tensions simmering before ultimately boiling over generated yet another layer of fear. I found myself terrified about sending my Black sons and daughters into a world where harm might come to them solely because of their skin color.

The insurrection at the Capitol building and increasing instances of domestic terrorism compounded these concerns exponentially. At certain moments, I felt prepared to abandon all peripheral concerns. Nothing seemed to matter beyond basic survival.

Thankfully, my rational faculties eventually reasserted themselves after adequate rest and conversations with my husband, who likely worried I was experiencing a genuine psychological break. Fear possesses the insidious ability to transform you into something dramatically less than your authentic self. It can shrink your entire existence down to a single point—survival mode—where nothing else registers as important.

Sometimes, in the quieter corners of my consciousness, I recognize a lingering fear of another challenging season approaching. However, I cannot permit such thoughts to consume me entirely because I retain hope for experiencing so much more goodness and beauty in this life.

The Rhythm of Seasons

These collective experiences consistently remind me how rapidly circumstances can transform…

One day radiates with sunshine,

Life feels abundant and promising,

And then, without warning, everything turns cold,

Difficulties multiply and darkness descends.

The remarkable aspect, however, is that neither condition endures perpetually. During the darkest moments of night, it certainly feels unrelenting. But we must remember that snow eventually melts, and heat inevitably dissipates.

Seasons change…
Storms arrive with intensity,
We continue living despite them,
We experience mortality,
We enjoy vibrant health,
We occasionally face illness,

But ultimately, healing occurs… even if healing means transitioning into the arms of Jesus.

Considered holistically, life simultaneously embodies beauty and terror. These reflections simply represent my contemplation of life's inherent paradoxes. The profound truth I've discovered is that experiencing fear doesn't negate the possibility of demonstrating courage concurrently.

You might reasonably ask why this matters.

Here's my perspective…

Fear: Not a Stop Sign

Fear doesn't function as a stop sign demanding complete stillness. It's more like a flashing yellow light—proceed with caution, stay alert, but keep moving forward.

Throughout history, fear has served as an instinctive protection mechanism, alerting us to potential dangers and triggering our fight-or-flight response. This biological reaction helped our ancestors survive predators and environmental threats.

However, in our modern context, fear often extends beyond immediate physical dangers to encompass concerns about failure, rejection, uncertainty, and a multitude of other psychological threats. It's like our fear response got an unwanted upgrade—same hardware, but way too much new software running in the background.

When I reflect on my daughter's health crisis, I realize that fear actually served as a catalyst rather than an impediment. It heightened my awareness, sharpened my focus, and ultimately propelled me toward taking necessary action despite my internal resistance. The paralysis I initially experienced gave way to fierce advocacy once I recognized what was truly at stake.

Similarly, my entrepreneurial journey required navigating through layers of fear—fear of financial instability, fear of public criticism, fear of failing while already managing significant life challenges. Yet had I allowed these fears to dictate my decisions, I would have missed discovering capabilities within myself I never knew existed. My business became not just a professional venture but a sanctuary of purpose during a profoundly challenging personal season.

The pandemic stripped away illusions of control we collectively maintained. No amount of planning, saving, or preparation could have fully insulated us from its impact. This global experience forced me to distinguish between productive and unproductive fears.

Washing hands diligently and maintaining physical distance? Productive responses to legitimate concerns. Spiraling into apocalyptic thinking and catastrophizing about every possible outcome? Counterproductive and emotionally damaging. (And yet I still did it regularly because I'm human, and humans are exceptional at imagining worst-case scenarios in vivid, technicolor detail.)

Questions That Turn Fear Into Information

What I've come to understand about fear is that it demands acknowledgment but not unquestioned obedience. When

I feel afraid, I've learned to ask myself several essential questions:

Is this fear protecting me from genuine danger, or is it merely protecting me from growth?

What specific outcome am I actually afraid of?

What's the worst realistic scenario, and could I survive it?

What opportunities might I miss by surrendering to this fear?

These questions help transform fear from an overwhelming force into useful information—data I can evaluate rather than commands I must follow. It's like turning fear from a dictator into an advisor who gets a vote but not a veto.

The racial tensions and social unrest created perhaps the most complex fear landscape to navigate. Unlike personal challenges, where action paths seem clearer, systemic issues generate fears that cannot be addressed through individual effort alone. I couldn't single-handedly guarantee my children's safety in a world where racial bias persists. This realization initially felt debilitating.

Over time, I've discovered that communal approaches to fear often provide what individual strategies cannot. Connecting with other parents sharing similar concerns, engaging in community advocacy efforts, and having honest conversations about race with my children all helped convert paralyzing fear into constructive engagement. Fear directed me toward community when individual action seemed inadequate.

Fear Is a Terrible Fortune Teller

The most significant shift in my relationship with fear has been recognizing its inability to predict the future accurately. Fear consistently presents worst-case scenarios as inevitable outcomes, but experience has repeatedly demonstrated that my fearful predictions rarely materialize exactly as imagined.

Even when difficult circumstances do arise, they never unfold precisely as my anxious mind anticipated, and I generally discover resources within myself and my community that fear failed to account for. Fear is basically the world's worst psychic—making dramatic predictions that almost never come true exactly as forecasted.

So, confront your fears directly but refuse to nourish them with unquestioned belief. Acknowledge their presence without granting them authority over your decisions. Remember that courage isn't the absence of fear but action in its presence. And perhaps most importantly, recognize that your fears don't define you—your response to them does.

Fear will always be part of the human experience—it's hardwired into our biology and unlikely to disappear entirely. But we get to decide whether fear serves as our commander or our companion. We can let it dictate our choices and shrink our lives, or we can acknowledge its presence while still moving toward what matters most to us.

The scaredy-cat who once hid under pillows during storms has learned that life's most meaningful experiences often lie on the other side of fear. Not because the fear disappears but because I've learned to bring it along for the ride without letting it drive.

Whatever fears you're facing today—whether they're shouting at the top of their lungs or whispering quietly in the background—know that you can acknowledge them without surrendering to them. You can feel afraid and still move forward. You can tremble and still be brave.

After all, courage isn't about being fearless—it's about

continuing to move forward even with shaking knees and a racing heart. And that kind of courage? That's within reach for all of us, even the self-proclaimed scaredy-cats.

The Underbelly of Pride

pride *noun* \ ˈprīd \ the quality or state of being proud

I vividly remember a day several winters ago. I was pregnant (you'll find that to be a common theme with me—apparently, I make major life decisions and have my most dramatic moments while growing humans). I had an attitude with my husband. The reason is not really important because I can't remember it anyway—which should tell you just how "important" it actually was.

My point is, I was upset. Not just regular upset, but pregnancy-hormone-fueled, righteous indignation upset. I was so upset that I made it up in my mind that I was not speaking to him at all. And especially not while he drove me to work because I was too afraid to drive in the ice and snow. Yes, I needed his help, but I wasn't about to acknowledge that fact. The silent treatment seemed like the perfectly reasonable response to whatever terrible offense he had committed (that was so terrible I can't even remember it now).

Before we even left, I'm in the house loudly gathering my things and taking them to our vehicle. Item by item I took them while we waited for our grey Chevy Silverado to warm up. I was making SURE he heard me stomping around, slamming drawers, and sighing dramatically. You know, really mature stuff.

He is clearly unbothered by my mood and that makes me even more determined NOT to speak to him. How dare he not be affected by my silent treatment? The audacity! He gets up to go to the car and I follow, but not closely. I'm not even going to give him the pleasure of walking me safely to the door. And why would I? I have made several trips by myself and I can absolutely do it again by MYSELF.

He safely makes it inside the truck and as I approach the passenger door, my foot meets a slick spot and I go tumbling down and under the Silverado.

Yep. I slid right under there. Like, fully under the truck. Not just a little stumble or a cute slip that he could have helped me recover from. Nope. One second I was vertical and righteously angry, the next I was horizontal and staring up at the undercarriage of our truck.

He didn't see me and I was way too prideful to shout out for help. Because I'm mad, and I've got to keep this up all day long. Remember? So I do what any sensible woman would do. I muster up every bit of adrenaline and get myself up and in the passenger seat without a peep.

You better believe I was hurt. My ego and my ass hurt. Bad. But I wasn't going to give my husband the glory of knowing my pride knocked me right on my backside. No freaking way! So I sat with it. The pain and everything while he goes on UNBOTHERED.

And that's the gotcha. I thought I was really doing something by imposing the silent treatment and not letting the gas out of my hot air balloon. I could have really hurt myself and my unborn baby. Thankfully, that didn't happen and I didn't make it out of the truck without bursting into uncontrollable laughter at the notion that I had not only fallen but slid under the truck all without my husband noticing.

There I was, sitting in the passenger seat, trying to maintain my angry face while simultaneously fighting the urge to laugh at the ridiculousness of what had just happened. The mental image of myself—pregnant, angry, and sprawled under a Chevy Silverado—finally broke through my pride-induced fortress. How can you stay mad when life literally knocks you off your high horse (or in this case, under your high truck)?

Pride: The Double-Edged Sword

Pride isn't bad. No. In fact, I have pride. Pride in my work. I have pride in who I am. I think it is having too much pride that can make for undesirable situations like staring at the underbelly of a car when you should be sitting in the passenger seat. That part.

Or being too proud to ask for help. Or, too proud to be the first one to apologize. That helps no one.

I've had many "too proud" moments and they've all ended up with me feeling pretty foolish afterward. Reflecting on some of those memories are even painfully embarrassing. Imagine falling just like I did but in front of a large crowd. That's what the replay is like when I recall my most prideful moments. It isn't at all fun, but I think my inner being is trying to send reminders of the payoff of pride. Kind of like my "don't go there" sensor. It's saying "remember what happened last time you got too prideful?"

There's a proverb that says, "Pride goes before destruction, and folly before a fall" (Proverbs 16:18). Not quite sure about the 'folly' part, but I can definitely relate to the pride piece. And I'm not getting all churchy, so don't even try it. I'm just making a quick reference in case you want to verify if what I'm saying has any credibility. It does. And you can try it if you'd like, but if I were you, I'd trust me. God has a special way of humbling the prideful, usually in the most embarrassing ways possible.

I haven't really arrived at the place where I've mastered the art of having balance in this area. But I have come to a realization that it's not pride that's the issue. It is my overutilization and misuse at times. Sort of like chocolate cake—a slice is delightful, but eating the whole thing will leave you with regrets and possibly lying on the bathroom floor questioning your life choices.

When Pride Takes the Wheel (And Drives You in Circles)

This incident with the truck wasn't the first time my pride had landed me in an uncomfortable situation, and it certainly wouldn't be the last. Pride has a way of creeping into our lives, often disguised as strength or self-respect, until suddenly we're staring at the underside of a metaphorical truck.

There was the time I refused to ask for directions when I was already twenty minutes late for an important meeting. I drove in circles, convinced I could figure it out myself, while my anxiety steadily climbed. When I finally arrived, flustered and apologetic, I made up an excuse about traffic rather than simply admitting I got lost.

Why? Pride. The thought of acknowledging my directional shortcomings felt somehow more painful than the actual consequences of being late. As if saying "I got lost" would somehow reveal a fatal character flaw that would forever alter how others viewed me. Looking back now, I realize no one would have cared—or even remembered—if I'd just said "Sorry, I got turned around and couldn't find the place." But in that moment, my pride convinced me that admitting a simple human error was completely unacceptable.

Then there was the business opportunity I nearly missed because I was too proud to reach out to someone who had previously rejected one of my proposals. I sat on it for weeks, letting pride convince me that making contact would appear desperate or weak. My inner monologue was like, "They already said no once. If you call them again, they'll think you're pathetic and can't take rejection."

When I finally swallowed that pride and made the call, the person was not only receptive but enthusiastic. My pride had nearly cost me a significant professional relationship. And you know what? They didn't even remember rejecting my previous proposal! The thing that had been living rent-free in my head for weeks wasn't even on their radar.

The pattern became clearer as I reflected on these experiences. Pride often masquerades as self-protection, but in reality, it frequently operates as self-sabotage. It's like hiring a bodyguard who ends up punching you in the face.

Pride and Prejudice (Mostly Against Myself)

In my marriage, pride has been both a shield and a barrier. Like most couples, my husband and I occasionally hurt each other's feelings or have disagreements. In healthy moments, we communicate, apologize, and move forward. But when pride enters the equation, what should be simple becomes complicated.

A simple misunderstanding that could be resolved with

a five-minute conversation instead stretches into days of tension because neither person wants to be the first to extend an olive branch. It's like we're both standing on opposite sides of a tiny creek, refusing to step across because we each think the other person should get their shoes wet first.

I remember one particular argument that stretched on for nearly a week. I was convinced I was right and deserved an apology. He likely felt the same way. We moved around our home like satellites in careful orbit, never colliding but never connecting. The distance was palpable and painful, but pride kept us locked in our positions.

When we finally talked, the issue was resolved within minutes, making the days of silence seem ridiculous in retrospect. The time wasted could never be recovered—all because pride convinced us both that backing down meant losing. As if marriage is a competition with winners and losers, rather than a partnership where either both people win or both people lose.

Watching Pride Through a Mother's Eyes

I've been thinking a lot about this duality since having children. When my daughter, Rhema was born, I watched her develop her personality with complete wonder. Even as a toddler, she had a fierce independence that reminded me of myself.

I admired her determination—the way she insisted on pouring her own juice (creating spectacular messes) or climbing onto furniture without help (resulting in several heart-stopping moments). But I also noticed how that same determination sometimes prevented her from learning new skills or accepting assistance that would ultimately help her achieve her goals.

It was like looking in a mirror. How many times had I created metaphorical messes or made things harder for myself because I was too proud to accept guidance? Watching my daughter navigate this tension between independence and interconnection has helped me better understand my own relationship with pride.

It's much easier to see the folly of stubborn pride when you're watching someone tiny refuse help and then spill juice all over themselves than when you're the one insisting you can handle everything alone. Children have a way of showing us ourselves in the most unfiltered ways.

Finding the Balance: When to Hold Pride and When to Let It Go

I think this is the distinction I'm still learning: the difference between pride that lifts us up and pride that holds us back. Healthy pride gives us the confidence to pursue our goals, stand firm in our values, and celebrate our accomplishments. It acknowledges the worth and dignity inherent in each of us.

Unhealthy pride, on the other hand, prevents growth, damages relationships, and keeps us isolated in our own self-sufficiency. It's the pride that would rather suffer in silence than ask for help, that would rather be right than reconciled, that would rather maintain appearances than admit vulnerability.

The older I get, the more I recognize how much energy I've expended defending my pride. All those times I pretended to know answers instead of asking questions, all the opportunities missed because I was too proud to take a risk and possibly fail, all the connections stunted because I couldn't bring myself to be vulnerable—the cost has been substantial.

It's like I've been carrying around this heavy backpack full of rocks labeled "appearances," "being right," and "not showing weakness." No wonder I'm tired! And for what? So people will think I have it all together? News flash: no one does, and most people can see through the façade anyway.

Yet I also recognize the value in the healthy pride that has carried me through difficult seasons. The pride that helped me persevere when others doubted my capabilities, the pride that motivated me to set high standards for my work, the pride that taught my children to value their heritage and identity—these expressions of pride have served an important purpose.

Learning to Laugh at Myself (It's Either That or Cry)

So perhaps the goal isn't to eliminate pride but to refine it. To develop the discernment that knows when pride is supporting our highest good and when it's hindering it. To cultivate the humility that can laugh at ourselves when we end up under trucks or creating unnecessary complications in our lives.

I'm working on recognizing the early warning signs of unhealthy pride in myself: defensiveness when receiving feedback, reluctance to ask for help, competitive feelings toward others' successes, the impulse to hide mistakes rather than learn from them. When I notice these signals, I try to pause and ask myself what I'm really protecting and whether that protection is serving me.

I've also started practicing small acts of pride-setting-aside: asking questions when I don't understand, admitting when I'm wrong, accepting help when it's offered, sharing my work before it feels perfect. Each small action helps recalibrate my relationship with pride.

And yes, I now laugh with my husband about the truck incident. It's become one of those stories we tell at gatherings, a reminder of how pride can literally and figuratively knock us off our feet. Because ultimately, the ability to laugh at ourselves might be the most effective antidote to unhealthy pride we can develop.

I'm still a proud woman. I still value dignity, self-respect, and excellence. But I'm learning that true strength isn't found in never falling or never needing help. It's found in the courage to get back up, to extend a hand, to say "I'm sorry" or "I don't know" or "I need you." That kind of courage requires us to hold our pride lightly, to know when to stand firm in it and when to set it aside.

So the next time you find yourself staring at the underbelly of a metaphorical truck (or a literal one—no judgment here), remember you're not alone. We've all been there, bruised egos and all. The question isn't whether we'll experience pride-induced falls, but how quickly we'll learn from them and how willing we'll be to laugh at ourselves in the process.

And maybe, just maybe, if we can learn to laugh at our own prideful moments, we can create spaces where others feel safe enough to be imperfect too. Because a world where we can all acknowledge our humanity—our mistakes, our needs, our occasional face-plants under trucks—is a world with a lot more connection and a lot less suffering in silence.

So here's to pride—the good kind that lifts us up, not the stubborn kind that knocks us down. And here's to laughing when we fall, because sometimes that's the most graceful way to get back on our feet.

Failed It, Nailed It

There's this show on Netflix that I love. It brings aspiring bakers together in competition to recreate some of the most amazing baked goods in the world. What is most enjoyable about this show is the replication. They almost always look nothing like the original. Beats me all the time and brings me so much joy.

Their failures are celebrated. It's not expected to be the perfect baker. As a matter of fact, the worse it is, the better. It's like watching a beautiful disaster unfold in real-time, and somehow, magically, it makes me feel better about every cake I've ever made that looked like it survived an earthquake.

We live in a society where failure is frowned upon when you're young. Yet, it is almost encouraged when you're older. It's so backward to me. So when you're young, they'd say 'You're a failure.' Then when you're older, they excuse you with remarks like; 'Fail forward, fail fast, fail often'.

My Epic Battle with College Algebra (Spoiler: Math Won... Until It Didn't)

After nearly a decade (or more) of attending college off and on, I finally earned my Bachelor's degree. It wasn't without challenge. I'm the one who waited until the end to tackle my least favorite subject: Math. Let me be more specific: College Algebra.

Who made the rule that we all need College Algebra to function in society? That's what I'd like to know. I'd like to have a strongly worded conversation with whoever decided that manipulating letters and numbers together was a skill all humans must master before being declared educated. Because I have some THOUGHTS.

I remember taking it for the first time. I left the first class with my head spinning. The formulas and letter-number combinations were torture. I mean why? Just why College Algebra? Who even invented it? Couldn't we all just do without it? I was sitting there thinking, "When in my adult life am I ever going to need to know what y equals when x is 7?" Spoiler alert: the answer so far has been NEVER. Makes Terrance Howard sound a little more reasonable if you ask me.

On one of my failed attempts at this class, I listened to a friend who told me that taking the class online was a breeze. That I only needed to score well on three of the four exams and the homework didn't count. Or at least that's what I thought I heard.

And that idea would have worked if I hadn't bombed three out of the four exams and skipped nearly all of the homework. Turns out that doing your homework really does matter; especially when you need a frame of reference when taking the exam. Who knew? (Apparently everyone except me.)

Failed it.

In my next attempt at college Algebra, I was trying to navigate through having a very sick child and focusing on passing a class that I loathed. Yeah, that isn't exactly a recipe for success. I was not only emotionally compromised but I also flat out did not want to do the math.

Of course, I could blame that fail on my daughter's illness but that is only part of the whole picture. Remember telling a story right? The other part was that I still had a mental block the size of Texas when it came to this subject. My brain simply refused to cooperate when numbers and letters started dancing together on the page.

Failed it. Again.

I was determined to be done with Algebra once and for all so I did what I probably should have done in the first place. I couldn't let myself be shamed by one subject without a fight. So here's what I did to salvage myself; I registered for the class in person and I took it seriously this time.

I did my homework and I studied. I did it all right this time. I wrote down every formula. I asked questions when things weren't clear. These are things that contribute to passing grades folks. (Revolutionary concept, I know.) And It paid off.

Nailed it.

The lessons are implied and I don't think I need to spell them out for you. But in case you're like me and need a few breadcrumbs, I'll break it down for you. Sometimes the simplest solutions are the ones we avoid the longest. Sometimes we have to stop looking for shortcuts and just do the work. Sometimes we have to admit that the problem isn't the subject or the teacher or the circumstances—it's our approach.

When My Olympic Dreams Came Crashing Down (In Spectacular Fashion)

I wish I could say that was my only experience with failure. It's not. Not by a long shot. My life has been a highlight reel of spectacular fails interrupted by occasional successes. It's just that the fails make for much better stories.

When I was in high school, I had an athletic body. More like a runner's body. Long legs, thin frame. Therefore, I was recruited in my sophomore year to run track. Once again my wild imagination painted me as Flo Jo. In my mind, I was the best thing that ever happened to the team. They were lucky to have found me.

That self-confidence may have been over-bloated but that was exactly how I felt. I was the best. Simple. I was already mentally designing my Olympic uniform and practicing my victory wave for when I inevitably broke world records and made my country proud.

I can still remember my first race. It was the open 400-meter dash. I had trained for that moment. I had new-to-me track shoes and a fresh uniform. I did all my warm-ups and conditioning. My family was there to cheer me on. Everything was in place. It was an incredible feeling.

I was nervous but I wasn't going to let that show. This was my moment to show everyone what I could do, that I could be the best. My dad had never seen me run before so I was excited for him to see his little girl win. I pictured him telling everyone the next day about his daughter, the track star.

My heart was racing and my palms were sweaty. I walked to my lane and did a light jog to shake some of the nervousness out. I scanned the crowd for my family AKA my cheerleaders and when I spotted them, I made my way to the blocks. I backed into the blocks just like I had seen on television.

I rocked from side to side until the man with the gun said "runners to your mark". Then I got still. Everything around me was silent. I blocked everyone and every sound out. I thought to myself that I was going to beat everyone in this race. I was mentally rehearsing my victory interview.

BOOM!

The sound of the gun signaled it was time to go. Off I went as fast as my feet could carry me. I started off in the lead. Everyone was behind me and that felt so good especially when it was my first time running. At about the 150 meter mark something happened.

That initial burst of energy was leaving my body. Do you know the way a pin pierces into a blown balloon or the way a sharp object punctures into a car tire and the air in it starts to deplete, fast? Exactly! That's how I felt my energy seeping out of me.

It felt like someone placed a book bag of bricks on my back and expected me to run full speed. How was that going to be possible? Suddenly, my legs weighed approximately 500 pounds each. Every step was an Olympic event in itself.

The finish line looked ten miles away. Woosh! One person passed me. Then another, and another. By the grace of God, I made it to the second curve and the final leg of the 400 meters. By that time I was doing a light jog. You know the kind that you might as well walk because you'd be going faster…that kind.

I heard my parents in the distance saying "Run Rachel! Run!" And I just could not. I heard my coach screaming "You better not walk Eggerson!" I wondered briefly if I could fake a dramatic injury to save face, but even that required energy I no longer had.

I. Just. Could. Not.

Ladies and gentlemen, for my first race I walked the last steps across the finish line dead last. And no it wasn't alright. It wasn't. Humiliated and exhausted I was. Couldn't look at my family. Couldn't run over to my teammates. How could I, anyway? That 400-meter dash kicked my ass. My dreams of Olympic glory disappeared faster than my stamina had.

Failed it.

You would think I wouldn't have been seen on a track again not even during PE. Trust me, those thoughts crossed my mind. However, I felt redemption was necessary. The only way to see that was to stick it out.

While I didn't ever reach Flo Jo or Sha'Carri Richardson status, even in my own mind, I did go on to find my flow. I ran hurdles and even the 4x4. I wasn't a full-ride scholarship track worthy but I wasn't bad either. And it was because I didn't allow myself to retreat after failing. I discovered that sometimes you have to recalibrate your expectations without abandoning the goal entirely.

Nailed it. Sort of.

These early lessons in failure were formative, though I didn't realize it at the time. Each experience was building something in me – a resilience, perhaps, or at least an understanding that failure wasn't final.

The track experience in particular taught me something crucial: starting strong doesn't guarantee a strong finish, and conversely, a difficult start doesn't mean you can't finish well. It's about pacing yourself, understanding your capabilities, and being willing to adjust your expectations based on reality rather than fantasy.

I think about that race often, especially when I catch myself starting something new with unrealistic expectations. The overconfidence, the lack of proper preparation, the misconception about what would be required – all of these mirror patterns I've seen in other areas of my life.

I entered that race with a highlight reel playing in my head, but reality doesn't work that way. Reality demands respect for the process, acknowledgment of limitations, and the humility to keep going even when you're not the star you imagined you'd be. Reality is what happens after your imaginary crowd stops cheering and your actual legs start burning.

When Entrepreneurship Knocked (And I Wasn't Exactly Ready)

Now, let's get down to business. By that, I mean the experience with starting my own. What is clear for me is that being my own boss is completely different from my original thoughts on it.

I used to think that if I'm doing "this" for a company, what's stopping me from doing "it" for myself and naming my price? I forgot that there's a different push when you know you can't fail another person because you answer to them. I thought I was in charge and did not have to answer to anyone but myself.

Wrong.

Trust me the push to perform is different. It's the difference between hitting the snooze button when you work for someone else versus when you work for yourself and every snoozed minute costs you money directly. It hits different.

I used to daydream about consulting but I didn't think that day would ever come, especially not the way it did. I guess you can say entrepreneurship kind of snuck up on me. Prior to taking the plunge, I was in corporate America. I had a solid career as a trainer and project manager.

I would only think of stepping out on my own when I got irritated on the job, passed over for a promotion, offered a lateral move which means more responsibility without the increase in pay. You know, those moments when you look around and think, "I could do this better on my own," while simultaneously being terrified of actually trying.

The thing is life presents: a sign. Always. I was six weeks post-partum and also caring for my daughter who had been in the hospital for a rare disease. Corporate had been as lenient as they could. To say they were understanding would be an understatement. They were very generous.

But business is business at the end of the day. Organizations don't stay in business by letting their employees work remotely right? At least, not prior to COVID. (If only I'd known a pandemic would make remote work the norm just a few years later—talk about timing!)

They needed me in the office or I could resign and return when my situation improved. My husband and I saw this as the opportunity I had been dreaming of. It was scary because who leaves a company with steady income and benefits when that is exactly what you need, especially at that time of your life?

However, I didn't see any other options. I couldn't leave my daughter alone and I had a newborn baby who also needed me. Sometimes life doesn't ask if you're ready for change—it just shoves you into the deep end and says, "Hope you remember how to swim!"

And so there it was.

I made the decision to go into business for myself.

The only thing is I didn't want anyone else knowing. I somehow thought that if my freshly former employer caught wind of me doing anything outside of sulking in a hospital and nursing a baby that they would summon me back to the place of complacency. And so I planned in secret.

And sometimes that's necessary. You don't need everyone knowing your every move. Not everyone deserves front-row seats to your life transitions.

I had a baby in January, quit my job in February, and planned a secret launch party for my business the following month. It wasn't the most conventional way of launching a business. But the point is that I did it. I. did. It! While most new mothers are trying to figure out how to shower regularly, I was planning business strategies between diaper changes. Looking back, I'm not entirely sure if I was brave or just delirious from sleep deprivation.

There was (and probably still is) something about forward motion in the middle of chaos and tragedy that helped me. I was fueled with so much energy to do, that, I didn't even give myself the chance to be dragged back by all that wasn't going right or easy.

The Launch Party That Wasn't (But Still Kind of Was)

I personally invited people to my launch party. I booked the venue. I had food catered in. I asked some of my connections to be vendors. I hired a videographer. I purchased hundreds of dollars worth of gift cards. Table settings. Party favors. Business cards. Pictures. I was in the red before my little business venture got started.

In my mind, this launch party was going to be EPIC. People would be talking about it for years. "Remember when Rachel launched her business? What a night!" It would be standing room only, with people clamoring to work with me right from day one. I'd probably need to hire staff immediately to handle the overflow of clients. That's how it works, right?

On the day of the launch, I could literally count the number of people who showed up on my hands (no toes needed) and most of them came from my womb or were related to me otherwise. But it didn't matter. I was embarrassed, hurt, confused, and had too much stuff to take home. I smiled through tears but inside I felt like a complete failure.

There's something especially painful about public failure—when you've told everyone to come see your moment of triumph and instead they witness your moment of humiliation. It's like falling on your face, but with an audience, catering, and professional photography to document it all.

After washing away my defeat at that moment, I began to think about how to rebound. Being an entrepreneur is so much more than a launch party. I had to get out there and create some business. Now here I am several years later still in business.

Nailed it.

This experience taught me something profound about failure: sometimes what we perceive as failure is merely a recalibration of expectations. I had imagined a packed venue, enthusiastic supporters, and immediate success. Reality delivered a humbling reminder that businesses aren't built on launch parties—they're built on persistence, adaptability, and consistent effort over time.

In retrospect, I'm grateful for that sparsely attended launch. Had it been a wild success, I might have developed unrealistic expectations about entrepreneurship. Instead, I learned early that this journey would require resilience, creativity, and the willingness to redefine success on my own terms.

The entrepreneurial path has been littered with failures large and small. There were proposals that never received responses, speaking engagements where I bombed, workshops where only a handful of people showed up, social media campaigns that generated zero interest. Each one stung in its own way.

Each one tempted me to retreat to the safety of traditional employment, where the parameters of success were clearer and the checks arrived on schedule. "Maybe I should just get a *real* job," became a regular thought during particularly challenging months. I even kept my resume updated, just in case.

But with each failure came an opportunity to refine my approach, to better understand my market, to clarify my unique value. I began to see these setbacks not as indictments of my worth or capability, but as essential data points guiding me toward more effective strategies.

What My Friend Failure Has Taught Me

Here's what I've learned from my dear friend failure. I have to accept that most days I don't know what the hell I'm doing.

But it's okay because I simply have got to keep moving. You learn on the job as you go.

It's like being thrown into the deep end of a pool and having to figure out swimming techniques while you're trying not to drown. Not ideal, but highly motivating and surprisingly effective.

I've got to pick myself up every. Single. Time. Especially when I don't even feel like it. On those days when staying in bed seems like the only reasonable option, those are precisely the days when getting up matters most.

I didn't have it all figured out before I began. I simply plunged in because I knew it was that or nothing. It's amazing that people like to hear from me still even after everything and the fact that I don't have it all perfectly figured out yet.

And that's the point. Life is a sprinkle of failures and successes. But the real point is this: never, ever stay down when you fall. Pick yourself up and do it again. Never wait till you're perfectly equipped before you begin. Don't be afraid of failures, just be grateful for successes, no matter how little they may be at the beginning, just keep on keeping on. It's like compound interest for your efforts—small consistent actions eventually create exponential results.

The Uncomfortable Truth About Failure
I know these:

Failure isn't fun because it sometimes robs you of the high esteem that you had spent a long time building. There's nothing quite like the humbling experience of thinking you're hot stuff one minute, and face-planting the next.

Failure isn't fun because it sometimes means hitting rock bottom and having to gather every bit and piece of courage you may have to start all over again. And starting over is exhausting, especially when you remember how much effort you put into the first attempt.

Failure isn't fun because it denies you of rest even after every effort you had exerted to make that thing work. When you fail, you don't get to rest in the satisfaction of a job well done—you have to immediately start figuring out what went wrong and how to fix it.

But I also know these:

Failure is sometimes the best teacher. How? It shows you the pitfalls you should avoid the next time you travel that route. Nothing highlights a pothole like falling into it face-first.

Failure is sometimes a teacher because it equips you with all the tools of knowledge you didn't have when you first began. You gain experience and insight that simply cannot be acquired through success alone.

Failure is sometimes a teacher because it tells you where you shouldn't exert your energy into the next time because it would be wasted. It helps you eliminate options and focus your efforts more effectively.

Failure is sometimes a teacher because it crowns you mentor in the same field you had recorded a *FAILED IT*. Now, you can show someone the best way to deal with the same situation you had failed in.

Your failures become your credentials in the most ironic way.

An Invitation to Fail Forward

So to anyone reading this who's currently sitting in the aftermath of a failure or rejection, I offer this: Feel it fully. Don't rush past the disappointment or pretend it doesn't hurt. Go ahead and have that ugly cry if you need to. Eat the ice cream. Call the friend who will let you vent.

But then, when you're ready, look for the lesson, the redirection, the opportunity hidden within the setback. Ask yourself what this experience is teaching you about your path, your preparation, your priorities.

Remember that every success story contains countless failures that never made the highlight reel. Every overnight success was years in the making. Every person you admire has a collection of rejections and failures they've metabolized into wisdom.

You're not alone in your failure. You're not defined by your failure. And just maybe, your failure isn't failure at all – it's simply a necessary step on your path to where you're meant to be.

So fail gloriously. Fail informatively. Fail forward. And then get up, dust yourself off, and try again—smarter, stronger, and with a better story to tell.

Finding Purpose in Rejection

Man's rejection is God's protection.

My mama says that to me all the time. It's her go-to comfort phrase whenever life decides to serve me a heaping plate of rejection with a side of disappointment. And while I love my mama dearly, I'll be honest—sometimes, when she says this, I want to roll my eyes so hard they might get stuck looking at my own brain.

Because let's be real—rejection stings. It stings no matter how prepared I am for it. It stings despite all the rational reasons why I shouldn't feel its bite. It stings even when I mentally armor myself with every positive affirmation and pep talk in my arsenal.

Rejection… it can mess with the best of us. It's a vulnerable place to be in because it's kind of embarrassing and it messes with your head in ways nothing else quite manages to do. It's like I'm silently asking; 'what is wrong with me?' But, I'm afraid to ask that out loud because… what if I'm told something that I don't want to hear? What if my suspicions are confirmed and I really am just not enough?

There's something uniquely painful about rejection that cuts across all types of personalities, backgrounds, and life experiences. Whether you're naturally confident or tend toward insecurity, whether you've experienced many rejections or few, that moment when someone says "no" to something you wanted triggers a visceral response that goes beyond logical thought.

When rejection hits, it rarely stays contained to the specific situation at hand. Instead, it tends to ripple outward, touching parts of our identity and self-concept that seem completely unrelated to the actual rejection. A turned-down job application becomes evidence of our overall unworthiness. A romantic rejection morphs into proof that we're fundamentally unlovable. A social snub transforms into confirmation that we don't belong anywhere.

It's like dropping a pebble in a pond, except the ripples don't just move outward—they somehow manage to find every single insecurity you've ever had and give them a little poke. "Hey! Remember that time in third grade when no one picked you for kickball? That's totally connected to this job rejection thirty years later!"

This emotional amplification happens partly because rejection activates our deepest insecurities and most painful questions. Am I enough? Do I matter? Do I belong? Is there something fundamentally wrong with me that others can see but I'm blind to? These existential doubts lurk beneath the surface of our daily functioning, and rejection has a way of bringing them roaring to the foreground, demanding answers we don't have.

The vulnerability that accompanies rejection is particularly uncomfortable in a culture that prizes strength, resilience, and independence. We're expected to "shake it off," to "not take it personally," to immediately locate the silver lining or lesson. These expectations create a secondary layer of shame—

not just the pain of rejection itself but embarrassment about feeling that pain so acutely.

We wonder why we can't be more stoic, more unaffected, more immediately able to see the bigger picture that others assure us exists. "Just move on!" they say, as if rejection hadn't just taken a sledgehammer to our self-esteem. Sure, Jill, I'll just "move on" from feeling like an utterly unworthy human being. Should take about five minutes, tops.

This complex emotional terrain makes rejection one of life's most universal yet isolating experiences. Universal because everyone faces it; isolating because we often struggle to admit its impact, even to ourselves. I've learned that acknowledging the sting—really feeling it rather than rushing to rationalize it away—is actually the first step toward genuine healing and growth. Naming the pain doesn't amplify it; it begins the process of integrating it into our larger story.

When the Professional Door Hits You on the Way Out

One of the more vivid rejections I experienced came when I was desperate. Things were going slow for my consulting business, and my husband's work was also slowing down. I was six months pregnant (I told you that would be a common theme), and I felt the pressure to provide equally for our household.

The timing of this particular rejection made it especially pointed. Pregnancy brings its own cocktail of heightened emotions, physical vulnerability, and financial pressure. There's nothing like the imminent arrival of a new dependent to sharpen your focus on economic stability.

Add to this the cultural messaging that pregnant women are less desirable employees (despite laws against such discrimination), and you have a perfect storm of circumstances to magnify rejection's impact. Because nothing says "hire me!" like showing up to an interview with what appears to be a basketball smuggled under your shirt, right?

My default is to look for a job. I figure that I have more than enough skills to bring value to any team. So, I started looking. And if you're thinking "I thought she was an entrepreneur. What is she doing looking for a job?" Listen, I will do whatever it takes to care for my family. I'll swallow every bit of pride and scan items at Costco if I have to and still run my business. Want to know why? Because sometimes, that is what it takes and actually Costco pays pretty darn good.

There's a prevailing narrative that true commitment to entrepreneurship means burning all bridges to traditional employment, that having a "Plan B" somehow demonstrates insufficient faith in your business.

This perspective always struck me as privileged and unrealistic, especially for those with dependents and financial responsibilities that can't be deferred while building a business. Sorry, kids, we can't eat this month because Mommy is committed to her entrepreneurial journey! Who needs food when you have #girlboss dreams?

The truth is that most successful entrepreneurs I know have, at some point, supplemented their business income with other work. Some maintain part-time positions throughout their entrepreneurial journey. Others take contract work during lean periods. Still others temporarily return to full-time employment when necessary before resuming their business pursuits. Heck, I'd still be working a corporate job now if I hadn't been laid off at the beginning of 2024. But God had other plans for me and at the moment I'm a full-time solopreneur, nonprofit founder, and when you read this you can call me Dr. Fox, because I'm earning a doctorate. Just thought I'd throw that in there (collar pop).

This flexibility isn't failure; it's strategic adaptation that actually increases the likelihood of long-term entrepreneurial success by removing some of the desperation that can lead to poor business decisions. It's the business equivalent of putting on your own oxygen mask before helping others—you can't build a thriving business if you're constantly panicking about basic survival.

Anyway, I digress. I submitted an application for two jobs that I was qualified for and had interest in. I got an email a few days after from one of them. I was assessed once then twice which is a good sign. Couple of days after that second assessment, I was contacted again for a phone interview. Another good sign.

The recruiter called and said I was moving forward with an interview in person. But before I got off the call, the recruiter wanted me to know that the position I applied for is no longer available. I was reassured that while this position was no longer being hired for, the hiring manager wanted to meet me. All good vibes and I'm feeling good about it.

This moment in the process—receiving positive feedback yet being told the specific role was no longer available—created a complicated emotional response. On one hand, the continued interest validated my qualifications and interview performance. On the other, the shifted goalpost introduced uncertainty about what exactly I was interviewing for.

The human mind craves clarity, especially in high-stakes situations like job seeking during financial pressure, and this ambiguity activated both hope and anxiety simultaneously.

It's like being told, "We don't have the dessert you ordered, but the chef wants to make you something special." It could be amazing… or it could be food poisoning.

My husband was making budgets with my new salary. Inside, I wasn't that confident that I had the job. Sometimes you have an inner knowing but your body just goes through the motions. I still held out hope that what I had heard wasn't exactly what it meant. Plus, the fact that I was 6 months pregnant never came up so there was that.

This discrepancy between external confidence and internal doubt is common during job searches. While my husband was already calculating household changes based on my potential new income, I was experiencing the intuitive hesitation that often serves as an early warning system.

We tend to dismiss these subtle internal signals, attributing them to negativity or anxiety, but they frequently represent pattern recognition happening below conscious awareness— our minds processing small incongruencies in the recruiter's communication, subtle shifts in tone, or other details that suggest misalignment. It's like your brain's spidey sense tingling, but instead of alerting you to danger, it's whispering, "Something's fishy about this whole situation…"

The fact that my pregnancy hadn't been discussed created additional cognitive dissonance. While it shouldn't legally impact hiring decisions, the reality is that many employers do factor pregnancy into their considerations, whether consciously or unconsciously. Want receipts? Ask the internet becasue I've lived it. The uncertainty about how this visible factor might influence the outcome added another layer of ambiguity to an already unclear situation.

I went in for my interview. I was confident because I usually interview well and this time was no different. It was like having a conversation with a couple of girlfriends. I was asked about my business and community involvement. I explained that I could easily manage this role without giving up those things. That didn't seem to bother the hiring manager.

The conversational, friendly tone of the interview created a false sense of security. When interviews feel more like casual conversations than formal assessments, candidates often let their guard down, interpreting personal connection as professional interest.

This dynamic can be particularly misleading for people (often women) who are skilled at building rapport and creating comfortable social interactions. What feels like successful relationship building may simply be pleasant conversation without genuine hiring intent. Just because someone laughs at your jokes doesn't mean they're going to give you a paycheck, unfortunately.

I also revealed my pregnancy that I didn't realize was so obvious from the side. I was told of the glorious benefits for moms. I was also told that they were trying to decide when to bring me on seeing they were kind of slow at that time.

From what I was told they *actually do* have a database where they keep *really great* talents like me that they pull from when opportunities come up. It sounded so good that I ate that bullshit for lunch. With a side of hope salad and a large glass of desperation juice.

The detailed description of maternal benefits and the reference to a talent database represent classic examples of what might be called "rejection redirection"—shifting the conversation from concrete job opportunities to vague future possibilities.

This approach allows employers to seem supportive and inclusive while effectively postponing or avoiding actual hiring commitments. The promised database rarely materializes into genuine opportunities, serving instead as a gentle letdown that preserves the company's reputation for supporting diversity and inclusion while actual hiring practices may tell a different story.

I left the interview feeling great-*ish*. I sent thank you emails. Like a boss, I was ready for my offer letter. Only, it never came. Radio silence. I was ghosted. By a potential employer. Not even a "thanks, but no thanks" email. Just... nothing. Cricket sounds. Tumbleweeds rolling by.

Deep inside, I knew they weren't going to offer me the job.

The contrast between external actions (sending professional follow-up emails, awaiting an offer) and internal knowing (recognizing the likely rejection) creates particular psychological strain. This divergence between what we hope for and what we sense is true forces us to hold conflicting realities at the same time—maintaining optimism while privately preparing for disappointment.

This emotional multitasking requires a ton of energy during an already stressful time. It's like simultaneously planning for both a wedding and a funeral, not knowing which one you'll actually be attending.

Weeks later, I got an email from the recruiter thanking me and telling me that I interviewed very well and they loved me. Only problem is they have pulled that role that I applied for. She assured me my resume would be floated around to other managers for interest.

It really crushed me but the flattening blow came a few days later when Indeed sent me a job listing for the week. Scrolling through them, I see a fresh post from the same place hiring for the same position I interviewed for several times. Damn! Now that was a sucker punch I didn't see coming.

This revelation—discovering the very position you were told was eliminated has been reposted—represents a particularly painful form of rejection because it adds dishonesty to dismissal. It's not simply that you weren't selected; it's that someone felt the need to fabricate a story rather than directly communicating that you weren't the right fit.

This lack of transparency undermines not just your confidence in this particular opportunity but potentially your trust in the hiring process generally. It's like finding out the person who told you "It's not you, it's me" is actually dating your exact doppelgänger a week later. The message is pretty clear: it was definitely you.

I kept going even though that hurt like hell. In my mind, I went through all the reasons why I wasn't good enough. My husband was pissed. I tried my best to bury this disappointment with all the others. I just didn't want to face it. The fact that I'm writing about this now is an accomplishment.

The mental exercise of cataloging all the possible reasons for rejection is both common and typically unproductive. Without concrete feedback (which is rarely provided), this self-analysis usually becomes an inventory of perceived personal deficiencies rather than an accurate assessment of the hiring decision.

This process rarely yields actionable insights but frequently diminishes self-confidence and increases anxiety about future opportunities. It's like trying to solve a mystery when all the clues are written in invisible ink and you're not even sure what crime was committed.

I stopped applying for jobs after that for a while. Having gone through the process, I know having a degree, exceptional skills, or ambition alone will not get you a job. It has to be the right job for you and the door that only God opens.

The truth is I wouldn't mind having a dream job. That would be living out my purpose and getting paid to do it. My dream job is one where I'm helping people, I'm writing, I'm speaking, and I'm doing what I love.

In a squeeze, I am guilty of forcing something that isn't my path. Because the truth is, if it is my path and someone wants me or what I can offer, they will seek me out. God is big, he opens doors. I've done my part. I only need to believe.

When Your Heart Gets Kicked Around Like a Soccer Ball

I've not only been rejected in my career, I've been rejected in relationships too. And let me tell you, nothing—and I mean NOTHING—prepares you for the special kind of pain that comes with romantic rejection. It's like career rejection's more dramatic, emotionally unstable cousin who shows up with a flamethrower instead of a pin.

I remember a time when I was dating. I met someone who I had become very close to. One evening, we were at a restaurant with a group of friends. He excused himself for a bit to use the restroom. Before he returned, another guy came out of the same restroom having spoken with this guy I was seeing.

This dude told me that the guy I was with said he never could get serious about me because I had "too many kids". Now, at the time, I only had three kids. I'm laughing so hard at this now seeing that I have ELEVEN! He said some other cruel and hurtful things that shattered my heart and confidence.

The kicker was, he was seeing someone in that same group of friends. The two of them left the restaurant together and I got stuck with the bill.

$13.75. Whew!

At least it wasn't an expensive heartbreak, right? Silver linings, people.

Relationship rejection carries its own particular sting, combining personal dismissal with intimate vulnerability. When we open ourselves romantically to another person, we reveal parts of ourselves typically kept protected—our deepest hopes, our insecurities, our dreams for connection and belonging.

Having these intimate disclosures met with rejection creates a compound wound: the primary pain of the rejection itself and the secondary pain of having one's vulnerability seemingly misused or devalued. It's like loaning someone your most prized possession only to have them return it broken—or worse, give it to someone else.

This particular relationship rejection contained multiple painful elements: learning about the rejection indirectly rather than through honest conversation; discovering the rejection was based on a fundamental aspect of your identity as a mother; realizing the relationship contained dishonesty beyond the rejection itself; and experiencing the small but symbolic indignity of being left with the bill.

Each of these components added layers to the rejection's impact, making it not just a romantic disappointment but a complex betrayal of trust and respect. It's like ordering a simple rejection but getting the deluxe package with all the painful add-ons included at no extra charge!

The seemingly incongruous detail of the exact bill amount—$13.75—highlights how rejection often burns specific details into memory. While larger aspects of the experience might blur over time, these small particulars often remain crystal clear, serving as emotional anchors to the experience.

The precision of this recollection underscores the impact of the event, while the relatively modest amount adds a note of irony that helps transform a painful memory into a story that can be shared without being completely retraumatized by the telling. Sometimes the absurdly specific details are what allow us to eventually laugh at our pain.

The rejections I've faced in my life that sometimes haunt me today still need work. They are some of the reasons why I sometimes don't feel good enough or feel that I am not enough. I came into the world that way. But just like I'm choosing to face it, we all have to at some point.

People have hurt me. I have also hurt people. An apology doesn't heal old wounds. Only God can do that. And it happens at the point of our surrender.

Fastforward to today and I am SO, and I mean SO extremely thankful for that rejection. Had it not happened, I wouldn't have been redirected to the love of my life, and now, almost twelve beautiful years of marriage, I can't thank God enough for that much-needed redirection.

Finding Your Power When Rejection Tries to Take It

The bottom line is this: I have to believe in myself even when I feel like no one else believes in me. When I've sunk so low, or when I've been rejected or received a bad review, I still have to believe that I've got something that no one else has. I've got a story worth sharing.

Self-belief in the face of rejection requires courage—not the absence of doubt but the willingness to coexist with it while still moving forward. It's recognizing that the negative voices (both external and internal) will always be present, but they don't have to be the loudest or most influential voices in your decision-making.

It's acknowledging that rejection's message—"you're not enough"—feels true in the moment without accepting it as an accurate assessment of your worth or potential. It's like hearing a convincing lie and saying, "That sounds plausible, but I know better."

Maintaining this perspective doesn't happen automatically. It requires intentional practice, supportive community, and regular reconnection with your deeper purpose and values. It might mean simply going through the motions on particularly difficult days until the emotional storm passes.

On better days, it allows for genuine confidence and creative risk-taking. Throughout all seasons, it serves as an internal compass that keeps you oriented toward growth rather than contraction, toward possibility rather than limitation. It's choosing, again and again, to be defined by your purpose rather than your pain.

All of this is less about me and more about who I'm supposed to reach, who I'm supposed to impact, even if it's just one person. So, I will not allow myself the time to sulk or feel so terrible. It's not worth it. It's not worth my time. It's not worth my attention. It may take a while but I am certain I'll come out stronger whenever rejections are dumped at my feet.

This doesn't diminish rejection's pain but places that pain within a larger context that prevents it from becoming all-consuming or identity-defining. It's like experiencing a painful fall while carrying something precious—your focus shifts from your own hurt to protecting what you're carrying.

The commitment to not "sulk" doesn't represent emotional suppression but rather intentional time-bounding of the grieving process. It acknowledges the natural need to feel disappointment while also recognizing that extended dwelling in those feelings diminishes capacity for both personal wellbeing and meaningful contribution.

I am certain that this is the moment I was made for; to bring God glory through my words, to show others that no matter what anything is possible.

Why?

Because I came into this world already enough.

The Beautiful Gift Hiding in Every "No"

The true measure of resilience isn't avoiding rejection or being unaffected by it, but rather developing the capacity to feel its impact fully while not allowing it to define your identity or derail your purpose. It's being able to say, "This hurts, and it matters, but it doesn't define me or determine my future."

It's using the experience as information rather than verdict, as redirection rather than roadblock, as temporary setback rather than permanent limitation. It's like taking a detour on a road trip—it might delay your arrival, it might be frustrating, but it doesn't mean you'll never reach your destination.

Each time we rise from rejection—whether through gritted teeth or genuine grace—we strengthen this resilience muscle. We build evidence that contradicts rejection's most dangerous message: that we are fundamentally inadequate or unworthy. We demonstrate to ourselves and others that worth isn't determined by external validation but by internal conviction aligned with meaningful purpose.

We transform what could be derailment into development, setback into strength, pain into purpose. It's like turning compost into garden soil—what begins as waste and decay becomes the nutrient-rich foundation for new growth.

In this sense, rejection becomes not just something to endure but potentially something to appreciate—not for its immediate pain but for its long-term contribution to who we are becoming. The doors that close direct us toward doors that open. The paths that end force us to discover new routes. The "no's" that disappoint ultimately lead us toward the "yes's" that fulfill.

This doesn't make rejection easy, but it does make it meaningful—an integral part of any authentic journey toward purpose and impact. It's recognizing that detours often lead to discoveries we would never have made on the main road.

So the next time rejection lands at your feet, remember: it's normal to feel its sting, to question its meaning, to need time for recovery. But also remember that its power is limited, its perspective partial, its verdict temporary. Something larger awaits on the other side of this pain—not despite the rejection but potentially because of it.

The very experience that seems to diminish you today may be developing the strength, insight, and direction you'll need for tomorrow. It's like resistance training for your spirit—the weight that feels heavy today is building the strength you'll need tomorrow.

As my mother wisely says, "Man's rejection is God's protection." In the moments when others say "no," something greater may be creating space for an eventual "yes" that aligns more perfectly with who you are and who you're becoming.

Trust the process, feel the feelings, and keep moving forward.

FINDING PURPOSE IN REJECTION

You came into this world already enough, and no rejection can ever change that fundamental truth. And sometimes, years later, you might even find yourself grateful for the "no" that initially broke your heart—because it ultimately led you exactly where you needed to be.

Permission to Filter

Let me give you a word of advice. Don't you ever, EVER ask someone what they think of you, unless, of course, you're ready to hear whatever they have to say. My emphasis is on the word **ready**. So, take note of that.

I know what you're thinking: "But how does someone really get ready for any response?"

That's the million-dollar question, isn't it? It's like preparing for childbirth. People can tell you all day long what to expect, but until you're actually in the delivery room with a tiny human trying to exit your body, you have no idea what you're in for. Opinions can feel just as painful sometimes, and no amount of preparation seems adequate.

There is a process of developing a thick skin that I believe only comes with time and experience. Writing about this brings back a memory about my favorite uncle, Uncle Lee. He had often come over to our home to visit. And whenever he did, he dominated the kitchen, making homemade biscuits and peach cobbler and all of the things no one on a diet should consume.

I loved it! Maybe that was why he was my favorite? No! It isn't. Uncle Lee is hilarious, he can sing his face off, he is a preacher's preacher, and he has the most unique way of telling a powerful story. He's the kind of uncle who walks into a room and suddenly it feels like the sun came out. You know the type—the relative who makes even the most boring family gathering worth attending.

On a particular visit, we were gathered around the table after eating ourselves into a mid-coma, thanks to Uncle Lee. For whatever reason, we began talking about relationships. My aunt reminisced about how she used to toss boys to the side like a piece of toilet paper when she was younger. What?! You can imagine how that felt for both my sister and I who had had our fair share of failed relationships and broken hearts.

There we were, trying to process the revelation that our sweet aunt was apparently the heartbreaker of her generation, while my sister and I were more like the heart-breakees of ours. Some family revelations hit different.

The Finger Story That Changed Everything

It was my uncle's turn to share and he stared at his hand and began to tell us a story about how he chopped off the tip of one of his fingers. I'll spare you the details of how or even why he did it because that's not the point. (Though between us, it involved a lawnmower, a rock, and what Uncle Lee calls "a momentary lapse in good sense.")

Uncle Lee explained how the pain was almost unbearable at first. Then it got so bad that he felt he had to go back to the hospital because he was sure he had gotten an infection or something.

The doctor told him something that sounds counterintuitive. He said that the pain was a sign that he was healing. Can you believe that? Wow! This is something he hadn't known before. Neither did I until then. He said that as time went on, his marred finger developed layers of skin over the wound.

He then took his finger and tapped it hard on the table. I'm not gonna lie, it was kind of funny to hear my uncle's finger tap resembling a pebble tapping on the dining room table. *Tap tap tap*. Like a tiny wooden drumstick. According to him, he didn't feel a thing and it is because he had developed so much skin over the wound that it no longer had the ability to cause him pain.

For someone who had had no idea about what my uncle explained, the phrase 'to develop thick skin' hit me differently from then on. It wasn't just a saying—it was a physical reality that perfectly captured an emotional truth.

So, let's do a brief recap so you get the connection between my advice and the story from Uncle Lee:

A part of the body felt some pain from a hurt.

The same part grew a tough enough skin to ward off any possibility for pain to ever exist as a result of that initial pain.

When You Ask *That* Question

Let's talk about something we've all thought about doing – asking someone "What do you think of me?"

Listen, I've got some real talk for you before you venture into those dangerous waters. Because trust me, I've been there, done that, and have the emotional battle scars to prove it.

Here's the deal: before you casually drop that question into conversation like it's not basically handing someone emotional dynamite with your name on it, make sure you're truly ready. And by ready, I don't mean "I think I can handle it" ready. I mean "I've done the inner work" ready.

This kind of readiness only comes after you've allowed yourself to really feel your feelings (yes, even the ugly cry ones), process through enough healing that your self-worth isn't hanging by a thread, and developed the kind of rock-solid self-awareness that can hear someone's opinion without it sending your entire identity into a tailspin.

Because without that foundation? Oh, friends. One slightly critical comment and suddenly you're on your bathroom floor, knees hugged to chest, wondering why on earth you thought this was a good idea while simultaneously counting the little squares on your bathroom tile through tears. Not that I've spent quality time in precisely this position or anything…

That Time I Thought I Was Oprah (Truth Bomb: She Was Not)

I admit it. I am an Oprah fan. I respect her so much and she's someone I have always wanted to meet. You know why? I think we have a lot in common. I mean, she's from Mississippi. I'm from Mississippi. She competed in pageants. I competed in pageants. She's a black woman. I'm a black woman. She has hair. I have hair. See?

Basically, we're practically twins. Except for the small details like her billion-dollar empire, worldwide influence, and the fact that she can buy a small country if she feels like it. But other than those minor differences, TOTALLY the same person.

Although I do not have a television show, yet, I've had a semi-active YouTube channel with a handful of videos. I've been on the news a few times but I am not an anchor like she is. I also remember a time when I tried my hand at hosting. It just so happened that the creator of a little local meet up believed in my ability to step into a hosting role.

The show took place at a local coffee shop. The host

and I met up a few times and he decided to hand over the opportunity to host an evening segment of this community attraction to me. And I was thrilled to accept. In fact, I had been eager to jump at many opportunities at that time.

I guess you could say that it was my year of Yes. In retrospect, it was probably my year of do-anything-to-keep-busy-and-not-face-the-full-trauma-of-a-very-sick-child. I would moderate panels. I would show up and facilitate workshops. I would attend networking events. You name it! As a matter of fact, anything I was invited to, I typically accepted.

And it didn't matter what it was. Whether it was a bar with a featured band I'd never heard of or an art gallery with an installation I can't even begin to explain, or a church service to sing for an event, it was a Yes, Yes, and Yes. Just sign me up!

My calendar looked like a toddler had gotten hold of a pack of colorful stickers and just went to town. It was a rainbow explosion of commitments, many of which I wasn't even sure why I'd accepted. But hey, opportunities, right (or distractions)?

Just like that, the first late-night show was set. Our first segment was a hot topic surrounding the Me Too Movement and I was set to moderate the discussion. No problem at all; at least none that I could foresee. I mean this is my thing right; my Oprah moment. I love to interview people, ask questions and get the juicy details for the people.

The setup was great. We had a lively discussion both on and off the stage. Our guests represented a male and female perspective.

Now, that was our first mistake. The gentleman on stage decided to speak up in defense of the men being accused in certain situations. He said that some women could be lying. In fact, there was even a semi-heated debate related to race and allegations.

And those in the crowd were not left out. Some of them yelled out their sentiments. Then of course we also happened to be streaming live on Facebook. Although comments weren't coming in at the time I do know people were watching.

On the whole, the night was a success. I mean we tackled a tough topic, right? Plus people were more than engaged. Some even went as far as staying after the show for nearly an hour. So, it wasn't too much that I went home feeling satisfied I believe. As far as I was concerned, this was the jump-off of my career in hosting shows.

I could practically see my name in lights. Move over, Oprah. There's a new host in town! I was mentally designing my future talk show set and picking out which celebrities I'd interview first.

Let Me Introduce You to the Comment Section

Let me give you another word of advice: Do NOT read the comments. I repeat: Do NOT read the comments.

It's like the digital equivalent of walking into a room where people are talking about you behind your back, except you've been given a special invisibility cloak so they don't know you're there. Nothing good can come from this situation. Nothing. Get out of the room. Burn the invisibility cloak. Run away.

I'm not sure what time it was but I do know it was either terribly late or very early. The persistent Facebook Messenger chime was going off. Unable to ignore it any longer, I reached for the phone to see a message intended for the creator of the show. I just couldn't help myself. I felt strongly that I had to read it.

I truly shouldn't have.

Why? It is because this message was a heated one explaining how appalling it was to have a male who clearly wasn't on the educational level of the female panelist. That a woman such as this (our female guest) should not have to share a platform with the likes of this man.

So, this message from Lord knows who, went on and on. As I read, my palms began to sweat, my feet as well. I didn't let myself stop. Rather, I went nervously to the video on the Facebook page then I looked at the comments. That was when the heat from all over my body escaped through my pores.

It's funny how we tend to narrow our focus and magnify the few horrible details said rather than the praise from the majority. I did exactly that! I zeroed in on the bad reviews and I didn't stop there. I took it personally.

I felt like every bad review was an indictment of my ability to facilitate such a delicate topic. And what was worse? I felt like I had somehow caused harm to the female panelist. I was unglued and no one had the ability to stick me back together. I felt embarrassed…humiliated even.

You know how in horror movies there's always that one character who decides to investigate the strange noise in the basement, and everyone in the theater is screaming "DON'T GO DOWN THERE!"? That was me, except instead of a basement, it was the comment section, and instead of a monster, it was unfiltered opinions about my hosting abilities.

I thought of the best way to salvage the situation; maybe try to undo the wrong. So, I reached out to the woman we had invited to the panel and asked if we could chat. She agreed.

By this time I was a miserable basketcase. By the way, I never wanted to host anything again. Forget that it was something I had always dreamed of doing.

When I got on the phone with the woman, I first of all apologized just in case I had made her feel uncomfortable by being on stage with the other panelist. I begged her to forgive me because deep down I truly hate disappointing people. It's a character thing. Not a flaw. It's just… a thing.

Well, our conversation went well and she assured me that all was forgiven and she wasn't the least offended. Whew! That felt good. I don't know how we got on the subject but somehow we landed at a point where I felt comfortable enough to inquire about her thoughts.

And the subject? Me.

The Moment I Should Have Just Hung Up the Phone

I asked her straight up what she thought about me. Now, don't forget that I didn't have a close personal relationship with this woman. Somehow, that didn't seem to stand out at the top of my mind.

To me, it simply felt enough that we had been mutually connected, somehow. And as for this woman? She gave me exactly what I asked for: Honesty.

I can't repeat verbatim what she said because that cannot be recalled from my head. However, what stuck out to me was that she said she found me to be someone who jumps at every opportunity (I'm paraphrasing).

I need to clarify that she was kind but boy was she direct? Yes indeed! This attitude made it easy for me to zero in on the one thing that I felt was the blow to my heart. Forget what she said exactly, what my brain heard and translated to my hurting heart was that; I'm all over the place, jumping at every opportunity thrown my way. What? And you know what? She was right. I was keeping myself busy and occupied to keep from falling apart.

It was no shock then that I literally DID fall apart inside. I thought to myself if she thinks this about me how many other people think this way? I cried to my husband who told me lovingly to get a grip. He also added that I might not be cut out for this type of work if I can't handle feedback. What? That's not what a loving husband is supposed to say, right?

Hold up. Let's imagine this scene for a second. There I am, tears running down my face, hugging a pillow for emotional support, looking at my husband with those "please fix this" eyes that spouses know all too well. And instead of the "Oh babe, she doesn't know what she's talking about" that I was fishing for, this man has the audacity to suggest I might need to toughen up? The betrayal!

Better yet, let's back up a bit. Why didn't this woman tell me what I wanted to hear? Maybe it's because I didn't actually ask her what my mind wanted to say and that was; "Tell me something that is going to make me feel good about myself". Instead what I asked for was the truth; her perspective.

And, how about my dear husband? He is rough around the edges and he doesn't tend to patty cake or coddle. He's not that type. Not really. So, when my hurting self came crying about someone's opinion about me, he stopped me right there, in a not so nice manner.

I was crying about what someone else thought about me, just this one person. And I won't even address that what I heard was almost guaranteed not what she said. I can promise you that. So, no! Don't even bother.

Unreasonably, what I had done was create the perfect storm of imagination where my debut hosting was a disaster and everyone on social media hated me and this woman also thought I was an opportunistic space cadet. That, my friends, was all me.

Understand this. I didn't need to take criticism of the show as a personal attack. I didn't need to reach out to that woman and invite her opinion into my life, especially when I wasn't ready for her response. I didn't know what to do with it.

I actually was out there floundering trying to find my place and jumping at every opportunity. To have someone even come close to pointing that out was too much for my tender heart.

I did not have thick skin.

I also didn't have a firm understanding of who I was or where I was headed. And, I think it's okay to not know. The only problem for me at the time was that I just didn't hold fast to this truth. It is because we are meant to evolve from one stage to another.

This experience taught me something profound about the relationship between feedback and self-understanding. When our identity is still forming – when we're not entirely clear on who we are or where we're headed – external opinions become disproportionately powerful. They seem to define us rather than inform us.

It's like building a house without first laying a foundation; every strong wind threatens to topple the entire structure. Or more accurately in my case, it's like decorating a house before the walls are even up. I was focusing on how others perceived me when I hadn't even established who I actually was becoming.

I've come to understand that developing thick skin isn't about becoming insensitive or disconnected from feedback. It's about establishing a solid core of self-knowledge that allows us to process others' perspectives without being destabilized by them.

When we're secure in who we are – our values, our purpose, our direction – we can receive feedback as information rather than definition. It's the difference between "this is an observation about something you do" versus "this is who you fundamentally are."

Looking back at my experience with that panel moderator, I recognize that my reaction wasn't just about her particular comment. It was about my own uncertainty. I was indeed saying "yes" to everything because I hadn't yet clarified what specifically deserved my "yes."

I was collecting experiences without a filtering system to determine which ones aligned with my purpose and which ones were simply distractions. It's like going grocery shopping when you're starving—suddenly, everything looks essential, and you end up with a cart full of random shit that doesn't actually make a cohesive meal.

Her observation actually contained a valuable insight that could have helped me refine my path – had I been ready to receive it. But at that point, I lacked the foundation of self-understanding that would have allowed me to use her feedback constructively. Instead, I experienced it as a wound rather than information.

When Performance Reviews Feel Like Judgment Day

Feedback is great as long as you are hearing what you want to hear. And that may be the comments that stroke your ego and praise you up. I remember dreading performance reviews. I mean I would rather do *anything* else than have a file pulled out to evaluate my work.

Actually, I was thinking of something terrible that I would rather do instead of sitting through a performance review, but my mind wouldn't allow it. I *would* actually sit through a performance review over having another baby with no pain medication. I *would* sit through a performance review over a root canal. And have you had a root canal? I did, and I would totally sit through a performance review over that.

On the whole, there are plenty of things that I *would* pick a performance review over, but I still don't love them. It's like voluntarily walking into a room where someone has prepared a PowerPoint presentation about all your flaws. "Let's begin with slide one: 'Areas for Improvement.' As you can see from this graph, your punctuality is on a concerning downward trend…"

It often feels like you're being called to the principal's office. Then you have that same pit in the tummy where you know you're not likely going to be fired, but there are probably areas that you're not so sure about, like showing up on time.

By the way, I always had a problem with that. My sweet spot was somewhere between 8:05 and 8:15, never 7 or 7:30 like my overachieving cube-mate. On a work day, every once in a while, I'd make it in the office before 8, and there she was typing away. Annoyingly perfect.

The company I worked for had called her out of retirement, as if Michael Jordan were coming to rescue the Bulls. Apparently, I wasn't enough to lead the training initiatives. She knew everything about the software because she was there when it was developed. She knew all the crazy complicated formulas that no one else could quite explain well.

Now, hiring her was exactly what my confidence needed. NOT. We would host training sessions with our clients. Sometimes we would tag team. Other times we would alternate. On top of that, we would send a survey asking for…you guessed it. FEEDBACK!

In fact, there was one specific workshop where I was admittedly on the struggle bus. There was math and formulas and if you know me, you know that my relationship with math is not that great. No, thank you! The feedback from the workshop was good overall. No harsh comments. Except one.

One person said "You should let the other one teach from now on. She's more knowledgeable." And friends, that comment, that ONE comment did me in! You hear me? I was crushed. I already felt some kind of way about the decision to hire someone else to work alongside me but now my worst fears were manifesting.

Everyone hated my training. I didn't know what I was doing after all. I shouldn't be there. You know, totally reasonable conclusions to draw from a single comment from a single person on a single day. Just normal, level-headed thinking here.

You do know that this was the talk I was giving myself and it became harder and harder to be motivated to perform at my best. And I blamed her.

Just look at her, coming in early and staying late, writing new material, and making videos.

I should be the one making videos. Pfuh.

Friends, something interesting happened while I was sulking over that one comment. My cubie took what she wanted. She ran right past me and, here's the kicker, I let her. I allowed that one comment to stop me from growing in that role and taking what I wanted.

The funny thing is, my boss never mentioned that one comment. It didn't show up in any reviews either. He obviously didn't seem to have noticed it. So, it was all me; in my head.

However, now that I'm in a different space, feedback looks a little different. I ask for it (if you can believe it). I welcome it now. I also have to be ready for the responses and…big gulp…take responsibility for the things. This may mean that I have developed thick skin. So, bravo!

Filtering Feedback: The Art of Not Taking Everything to Heart

This workplace experience illustrates another critical aspect of developing thick skin: learning to put feedback in its proper perspective. That single negative comment about my teaching effectively erased all the positive feedback I had received. Why? Because it confirmed the doubts I already harbored about myself.

It's as if we have internal radar that selectively detects and amplifies criticisms that align with our secret fears. It's like having a metal detector that only beeps when it finds precisely the thing you're most afraid of discovering.

I've learned that this selective hearing isn't unique to me. It's a familiar human tendency psychologists call "confirmation bias" – we tend to notice and remember information that confirms our existing beliefs while overlooking information that contradicts them.

If we secretly fear we're inadequate, we'll latch onto any evidence that supports that belief, no matter how minor or isolated. Our brains are basically little evidence-collecting lawyers building a case for whatever we already believe about ourselves.

Developing thick skin involves recognizing this tendency and deliberately working against it. It means forcing ourselves to give equal or greater weight to positive feedback. It means questioning our automatic interpretation of criticism. It means considering the source and context of feedback before accepting it as truth.

In the years since that crushing workshop comment, I've developed a more intentional approach to processing feedback. When I receive criticism that stings, I ask myself several questions:

Is this one perspective or a pattern across multiple sources?

Does this feedback align with my own observations about my strengths and weaknesses?

Is this feedback about a skill I can improve, or is it about an inherent quality?

What might I learn from this feedback, even if I don't agree with all of it?

How might I use this information to grow rather than to beat myself up?

These questions help transform feedback from a potential weapon of self-destruction into a tool for growth. They allow me to extract useful information while protecting my sense of self-worth.

I also remind myself that feedback often says as much about the giver as it does about the receiver. That workshop participant who preferred my colleague's teaching style wasn't objectively assessing my worth as a trainer – they were expressing a subjective preference based on their own learning style, needs, and biases.

Understanding this helps me depersonalize feedback that might otherwise feel deeply personal. It's like realizing that someone's preference for chocolate ice cream over vanilla isn't a commentary on vanilla's inherent value—it's just a personal taste.

Perhaps most importantly, I've learned to distinguish between feedback about my performance and feedback about my worth. They are not the same thing, though we often conflate them. A criticism of how I handled a specific situation is not a condemnation of my value as a human being or professional. Making this distinction is essential for developing the resilience we call "thick skin."

So where does this leave us? I believe developing thick skin is a lifelong process, not a destination. It requires ongoing self-awareness, intentional perspective-taking, and regular reality-checking of our interpretations. It demands that we build a solid foundation of self-knowledge that can withstand external opinions without crumbling.

And perhaps most importantly, it calls for self-compassion – recognizing that our sensitivity to feedback isn't a character flaw but a human tendency that we can gradually reshape with patience and practice. Being tender-hearted isn't something to overcome; it's something to protect and channel productively.

The next time you find yourself stung by someone's opinion or feedback, remember Uncle Lee's finger. Remember that the pain itself isn't necessarily the problem – it might actually be part of the healing process. And remember that with time and proper care, even the most tender spots can develop a resilience that allows you to tap them against the table of life without flinching.

You can have an open heart without having thin skin. You can receive feedback without receiving identity-defining wounds. You can filter opinions through the sieve of your self-knowledge, catching what's useful and letting the rest flow away.

And most importantly, you can give yourself permission not to absorb every opinion that comes your way. Some of them simply aren't meant for you.

The Quiet Roar of Courage

We moved in 2020 and one day I had finally gotten to open old boxes. You know that feeling when you're unpacking and find things you forgot you even owned? Like archaeological evidence of your former self? That was me, knee-deep in cardboard time capsules.

This one box had a bunch of notebooks and journals half-written in. Most of them I tossed in the giveaway pile. I didn't think that I'd be needing them anymore. "Goodbye, old grocery lists and abandoned to-do items from 2012," I thought.

Then I came across a green college notebook. Somehow it pulled my attention differently. It was like it had its own gravitational field, tugging at my fingertips. So, I opened it and there, on the first page I had listed the names of my children, their social security numbers, then what looked like a credit card number, and the name of a lawyer. Then, I also made some notes for myself.

The notes read:
Sent email this morning
He responded this afternoon
$500 + $145 filing fee
Find another place to live

Contact the bank and see if I can purchase a home

In the same book, I wrote some other thoughts.

I am going to check with Courtney's dad. I hope he has good news. Looking for a place to stay is hard. I am praying for favor. I want this part to be over already or at least to be separated. IDK. I just need space. This chapter in my life is just hanging. I want to stop wavering for once and go with something. I just don't want to be bothered by anyone.

And just like that the memories flooded back to me.

I was planning to divorce my first husband.

It hit me like a punch to the gut. That green notebook wasn't just paper and ink—it was evidence of the moment I finally found my courage.

When "Enough" Finally Means Enough

After years of abuse and infidelity, I was ready to take that next step and I was scared out of my mind. My hands were sweating. I had a nervous gut. I couldn't eat. All I knew was that I had to make this choice. This was not the first of it; I had been on the verge so many times but had backed away.

Like the time when he attacked me before work out of nowhere, threatened to kill me, and sent me running for my life, leaving the kids in the truck. Just the thought of it! That should have been the last straw and I thought it was for sure. I filed the charges against him. I got a new place for me and the kids. But! Something happens when you're in an abusive relationship that only those who have walked that path would relate to. It's like your heart and your head are in two different worlds. Your heart is so deeply connected to the person who hurts you. Meanwhile your head is having another conversation of knowing the exact next steps. The two rarely meet until the heart is finished. My family wanted me to be done. My dad, my hero, stood by me and encouraged me to stand and press charges. What he didn't know is that I had been speaking with my abuser and hearing all of his promises to change. Truthfully, I was still in love and I wanted our family to stay together. The day of court proceedings came, and I just couldn't go through with it. I dropped the charges.

I saw the hurt and disappointment in my father's eyes who left the courtroom before I could meet up with him. That hurt. I could only turn around and face the man who had been causing me so much pain. All I had to hold onto was the promise that he would never hit me again. Some time passed and the sting of the attack faded. Gratefully, some intense therapy contributed but the sting of that trauma is something I don't think I'll every fully forget. I remember the day my heart had enough.

Valentine's Day was coming up, and I was hopeful. Nothing had happened that I can recall, but I remember being worried. He hadn't come home after helping out at the church, and he wasn't answering his phone. I called the church to see if they were still working.

You probably know where I'm going with this one.

He hadn't been there. Surprisingly, I was calm—very calm—scary calm—the kind of calm that happens when your emotional system has basically thrown up its hands and said, "You know what? I'm taking a break. You're on your own for this one."

I waited for him to get home. He had this look on his face

that I had seen so many times. It's like the look a dog gives when they know they've done something wrong. You know the look—head slightly down, eyes up, bracing for the "What did you DO?" moment.

Then he gave this long-winded confession coated with fake tears. That was all I needed. I knew it was over. My heart had taken more than enough. I had reached my elasticity limit with him. And the papers hadn't been drafted or served. We hadn't seen a lawyer or been to court.

I was already divorced.

I had no tears left. I felt nothing. The nervousness I felt in planning came from the uncertainty of having a place to stay or finances to take care of my children. This time, the nervousness had nothing to do with me wondering if I could go through with being apart from him or leaving him.

This nervousness was different. It was all centered on what lay ahead, what I could do next, how I could do it—away from him; far far away. I had to sort so many things out and I didn't quite figure out how. Still I moved forward.

The Moment Courage Found Me

I took what little money I had saved, created a plan on paper with some scattered thoughts (but that didn't matter) and most of all, a made up mind. I remembered the words of a prophet who came to my parents' church. His words to me were clear. 'You can come out of the rain'.

It was as if I was being given permission to take my life back. It wasn't fun, and it hurt a lot. It was messy, but it was final.

But that's it right?

Sometimes courage is thought of in terms of how many lives someone saves or how someone narrowly escaped death. I even imagine someone jumping into raging waters to save a drowning child. You know, the stuff of superhero movies and viral videos.

But, courage is literally standing in the face of fear.

Courage is also walking away from an abusive situation and facing an unknown future. Courage lets you see positivity despite the uncertainty of the future. Courage seems to keep your eyes away from all the things that could possibly go wrong.

Courage doesn't let you bow to those legit excuses and calculations punching from different angles. Courage drums the singular truth in your ears; telling you that if only you can keep going, if only you can keep taking one step at a time, you'll see light.

The day I walked away from that marriage was the day I took my first real breath in years. I remember packing what I could fit into my car while he was at work. The children were confused, asking questions I couldn't fully answer yet.

I remember the weight on my chest, not knowing what tomorrow would bring, but knowing with absolute certainty that staying would bring nothing but more pain. That certainty—that clarity—that was courage speaking. It whispered, "Trust yourself. You know what you need to do."

And I listened. Finally, I listened.

Courage Comes in All Shapes and Sizes

It takes courage to do…almost anything and everything. There are moments in my life that require courage. Moments like standing up to a hospital system that repeatedly failed my child while she was going through a terrible disease. I knew I couldn't just sit around and let my daughter's fate be in the hands of those who saw her as a patient and nothing more.

Fear would have tried to make me believe that they were doing their very best. After all, they are the professionals right? At that time, fear whispered in my ear 'What do you know? You're just a mom? Don't overreact'. It would have been sensible or even logical to listen to that manipulative voice. But courage made me look past all of that and speak up. My child needed that.

I remember the day I firmly told the doctor, "We need a different approach." My voice didn't shake, though my hands did. The doctor looked at me with that practiced patience they reserve for "difficult" parents. You know the look—that "bless your heart, you've been Googling again" expression that makes you feel about two inches tall.

But I stood my ground. I had done the research. I had watched my child suffer through treatments that weren't working. I had listened to them try and explain her seizures as epilepsy. And when they tried to pacify me with medical jargon, courage helped me say, "I understand what you're saying, but it's not working for my child." That's when things began to change. That's when courage kicked in. I was tired of not having any answers. One night I saw a YouTube video of a young woman who was having the exact symptoms that my daughter was. The team kept dismissing me because they had already tested her for encephalitis but the forgot one thing. The titers. To this day, I know it was God who showed me what to ask the medical team to do. I told them to check here again and, this time, check the titers. Reluctantly, they did (likely to shut me up). What came back is what I had been saying to them for a while. She tested positive for Anti-NMDA Receptor Encephalitis. This is how her healing journey began, with the diagnosis she desperately needed.

Courage has to be ignited by fear. It probably wouldn't be courage if fear wasn't tugging at your sleeves asking you if you've lost your mind considering what you're about to do. It's like fear and courage are dance partners—you can't have one without the other showing up.

Courage is also activated by someone or something you truly love.

It's that fierce, protective love that calls forth courage we didn't know we had. When my child was in that hospital bed, I discovered reserves of strength I never knew existed. I became an advocate, a researcher, a voice that wouldn't be silenced. Not because I wasn't afraid—I was terrified—but because the love I had for my child was stronger than that fear.

When Being Yourself Takes Guts

Courage is standing up to microaggressions in the various spaces I take up as a black woman. For example, at work when someone questions my intelligence or ability. Courage is not holding back out of fear that I may lose work, friends, or other benefits. Courage is ignoring the warning that some may not like me for taking a stand. Courage empowers me to say I am strong enough to face whatever comes out of this. Courage makes me silence those voices that tell me that many others before me have failed.

I remember a time I was in a professional meeting when a senior leader referred to my tone as "aggressive" when I had simply spoken up for myself with the same confidence as my white counterparts. I felt that familiar knot in my stomach—the one that forms when you're deciding whether to speak up or let it go, the one that asks, "Is this worth it?"

But courage moved me to say, "I wasn't being aggressive; I was being direct and clear." The Zoom fell silent, but something shifted. Not just for me, but for those who believed I didn't have the right to speak up.

When we push past fear, when we refuse to be silenced or diminished, when we choose truth over comfort, we find ourselves—the real us, the person we were meant to be before fear convinced us to be someone else.

It takes courage to take up spaces where I am the only one of my kind. I stay because I know that maintaining that space is the right thing. I'm fulfilling a purpose. Courage keeps me believing that I'm no less than anyone else.

I've often been the only Black woman in the room—in professional settings, in academic environments, in social circles. There's always that moment of hesitation when you walk in. That split second when you consider turning around, finding somewhere more comfortable, somewhere you "belong."

It's that moment when you wonder if you should try to shrink yourself, to be less "you" so you don't stand out. Should I straighten my hair? Should I code-switch? Should I avoid bringing up certain topics? The mental calculations are exhausting.

But courage propels you forward. It reminds you that your presence matters, that your voice needs to be heard, that your perspective is valuable precisely because it's different. It whispers, "You belong wherever you choose to be."

The Kind of Courage That Doesn't Make Headlines

Sometimes courage is only attributed to the most outrageous things like walking into a burning building to save a cat. But, I think we need to look at the quiet courage. Quiet courage often goes unnoticed, uncelebrated. But it's the kind that changes the world. It's in the mother who works three jobs to give her children opportunities she never had. It's in the student who speaks up about bullying despite being afraid of becoming the next target. It's in the person who admits they were wrong and seeks to make amends.

These aren't dramatic acts that make headlines, but they're transformational nonetheless. They don't come with cape and spandex, but they're heroic all the same.

I think of the quiet courage I witness in my community every day. The neighbor who checks on the elderly woman next door, even though she's busy with her own life. The friend who tells you a truth you don't want to hear because they love you too much to let you continue down a destructive path. These ordinary acts of courage sustain us all.

The Courage to Change (Even When It's Terrifying)

It takes courage to not follow the trend or the crowd. It takes courage to stand out. Courage pushes me to step out. It is courage that propels me to allow transformation to happen. Courage to change. To be better. It is a force of life.

Transformation is never comfortable. It requires us to acknowledge that where we are isn't where we want to be. It demands that we face our shortcomings, our fears, our insecurities. It asks us to let go of the familiar—even when the familiar is unhealthy or limiting—and step into the unknown. That takes courage.

It's like being asked to jump out of a perfectly good airplane. Yes, there's a parachute. Yes, the view will be amazing. But also—YOU'RE JUMPING OUT OF AN AIRPLANE. The "before" might not be great, but at least you know what it is. The "after" is a big question mark, and that's scary as heck.

I think about the times in my life when I've transformed the most. They've always been preceded by discomfort, by a nagging sense that something needed to change. And they've always required me to be brave—to try something new, to admit I was wrong, to ask for help, to believe I deserved better.

Courage doesn't have an age or gender. Courage calls each of us. At times, you might be scared out of your mind. I hear you. I've been there, and it still happens. But if you dare to give into courage, you'll find yourself doing the impossible. If you dare to give into courage, you'll look back and say, "Whew! I did that? Yep. I did that."

And that's the beauty of courage. It's available to all of us. It doesn't discriminate. It's there, waiting to be called upon, ready to help us face whatever lies ahead.

The next time fear tells you that you can't, that you shouldn't, that it's too risky or too hard or too much—remember that courage is also there, ready to tell you a different story. A story where you are strong enough, brave enough, worthy enough to face whatever comes your way. A story where, no matter what happens, you can look back and say, "I did that. I had the courage to try."

In the end, that's what courage is all about—not the absence of fear but the determination to move forward despite it. And that, my friends, is a power we all possess. It might not roar like a lion, but that quiet voice of courage? It can move mountains, one brave step at a time.

Faith Refined by Fire

faith: complete trust or confidence in someone or something - **dictionary**
faith: the substance of things hoped for, the evidence of things not seen - **Bible**

Friends, can we talk about faith for a minute? Not the sanitized, Pinterest-worthy version that fits neatly on a coffee mug and looks cute on your shelf. I want to talk about the messy, tear-stained, sometimes-includes-words-you-wouldn't-say-in-front-of-your-pastor kind of faith. The kind that gets put through the wringer and somehow—miraculously—comes out stronger on the other side.

The dictionary defines faith as "complete trust or confidence in someone or something." So clean. So simple. And then there's the biblical definition: "the substance of things hoped for, the evidence of things not seen." Beautiful words, but honestly? Neither definition captures what faith feels like when your world is crumbling around you and you're desperately clinging to the belief that somehow, someway, things might possibly be okay again.

So grab your coffee (or wine, water bottle, or wine in a water bottle, no judgment here), and let me tell you what faith

ACTUALLY looks like in the trenches of life. Not because I have all the answers (surprise: I definitely don't), but because maybe—just maybe—my story might help you make sense of yours.

When Your Faith Gets Put Through the Industrial-Strength Spin Cycle

Remember how in movies, the main character always gets some dramatic warning before disaster strikes? Ominous music. Dark clouds. A wise old mentor saying something cryptic.

Yeah, I don't know about you, but my life doesn't work that way.

My daughter's illness—a terrible autoimmune disease that attacked her brain—came out of absolutely NOWHERE. One day we were living our normal, wonderfully boring life, and the next? Script flipped. No warning, no preparation—just a medical crisis that turned our world upside down faster than you can say "neurologist."

After weeks of hospitals and tests and treatments, we hit the point where the medical team basically shrugged their collective shoulders. I remember being handed these glossy brochures about a facility for patients with severe brain injuries. The photos showed beautiful gardens and smiling staff members. The medical team assured me my daughter would be well taken care of.

There was just one tiny problem: it was a 45-minute drive away. That meant either commuting daily or staying with her while my other children remained at home with my husband. I remember staring at those brochures thinking, "This is NOT how this story was supposed to go."

Can we talk about God for a second? Because I was ANGRY. In my mind, I had been doing everything right. I was the church volunteer queen! I showed up to every service! I prayed! I sang on the worship team! I was kind to strangers, animals, and even telemarketers!

I mean, isn't that how the Christian contract is supposed to work? I punch my spiritual time card faithfully, and God makes sure horrible things don't happen to my children? I'd kept up my end of the bargain—so where was the divine response? Where was the miracle I desperately needed?

I signed the papers (with shaking hands) and my girl was transferred to the facility. And let me tell you, friends, what we found was NOT what was in that brochure.

You know those horror movies where someone drops off their loved one at what they think is a nice place, but once they get there, it's straight-up nightmare fuel? EXACTLY LIKE THAT.

The walls were hospital-grade beige and institutional, nothing like the cozy, homelike images they'd shown me. The staff seemed stretched thinner than my patience after a week of homeschooling. The hallways echoed with sounds that definitely weren't in the brochure—moans, occasional screams, the constant beeping of monitors, and the squeak of rubber-soled shoes rushing past.

It was like ordering a five-star vacation package and arriving at a roadside motel with flickering lights and mysterious stains on the carpet. And yes, I've stayed in one of those motels, and no, I will not be sharing that story today.

Part of my daughter's illness caused her to scream most of the day and move constantly. It was as if she was trapped inside her own body, unable to communicate what she needed.

While family was with her, we could control what happened and advocate for her. I had specifically requested she not be restrained or given certain medications we'd already tried that were about as effective as trying to put out a forest fire with a water gun.

One time I returned from a quick store run to find her strapped in a car seat in her room. Another time I found staff holding her down and injecting her with the EXACT medication I had instructed them not to give her. "She became violent and uncontrollable," they said.

Funny how that never seemed to happen around me or my family. Maternal rage is REAL, people.

That was it. The final straw that broke this mama camel's back.

I remember driving home that day in tears—not cute, movie-star tears where one elegantly rolls down your cheek, but ugly, tears and snot-everywhere, probably-shouldn't-be-operating-heavy-machinery crying. I told God I couldn't do this anymore. I told Him exactly how upset I was, probably using some vocabulary that wasn't Sunday School-approved.

You know that conversation you have with God when you're at the absolute end of your rope? The one where all pretense of having it together flies out the window and you're just raw? That was me—looking like a horror movie extra, negotiating with the God at 65mph.

In those moments of despair, I questioned EVERYTHING I thought I knew about faith. Was it real? Did it matter? Had I misunderstood what faith *actually* means? Perhaps I had confused faith with a transaction—if I believe enough, God will give me what I want, like some cosmic vending machine.

But deep down, I knew faith wasn't a punch card system

where you get ten stamps and redeem them for a miracle. (Although, wouldn't that be CONVENIENT? I'd be saving mine up for a long and overdue vacation with NO children.)

When God Shows Up Wearing Casual Friday Clothes

What happened next wasn't the dramatic miracle I'd imagined with angels and trumpets. It was quieter than that.

My daughter was transferred to the hospital for a treatment she needed. While there, I vented to a doctor I'd come to trust, telling her I just wanted to bring my girl home. I wasn't even asking for anything—just emotional dumping all over this poor woman who probably had twelve other patients to see.

But sometimes God works through doctors in white coats instead of angels in white robes.

By discharge time, they were suddenly releasing her to come HOME with us. No dramatic healing, no heavenly choir— just a stack of papers and a tired doctor's signature. And isn't that often how faith works? Not with lightning bolts and dramatic music but with small openings, tiny shifts that create possibilities where none existed before.

I'd been waiting for the Hollywood version of a miracle— complete with swelling music and dramatic lighting. Instead, I got a quiet permission slip in a manila folder. Sometimes God's answers come via standard mail instead of special delivery with a bow.

Now, I'd LOVE to tell you she got better immediately after coming home. But if I did, my pants would literally burst into flames. It took EVERY member of our family pitching in. We had to feed her through a feeding tube, change her, bathe her, and make sure she didn't take off running down the street, which she did a lot—apparently, my daughter thought "escape artist" might be a good career option and sometimes she'd take an accomplice from our younger crew.

Each day felt like running a marathon in flip-flops. The constant vigilance, the physical demands, the emotional toll of seeing my vibrant girl so altered—all of it tested not just my faith but my endurance, my patience, and my ability to function on two hours of sleep and dangerous amounts of caffeine.

There were moments—I'm not afraid to admit—when I wondered if we'd made the right choice bringing her home. If we were equipped for this. If I was strong enough. Caregiver fatigue is REAL, friends—and it doesn't come with a user manual or an expiration date.

I tried EVERYTHING. I prayed harder than I've ever prayed. I used so much anointing oil our house could have been a slip-and-slide. I read the Bible out loud, played worship music 24/7, and she still didn't get better. I even took her to morning prayer service.

She was still running around the sanctuary screaming like we were at a heavy metal concert.

I'm pretty sure I went through every spiritual "treatment" in the book. I was like a faith mixologist—trying different combinations of prayer, scripture, worship music, and anointing oil, hoping to find the magic formula that would unlock healing. "Maybe if I add a splash of fasting with a twist of all-night prayer…" But no matter what spiritual concoction I tried, the results remained stubbornly the same.

And in those endless days, I learned something profound about faith. It isn't always about seeing immediate results. Sometimes, faith is simply the ability to take one more step when you can't see the path ahead. To keep moving forward when every logical part of you wants to curl up in a ball with Netflix and a Costco-sized bag of Doritos.

When the Miracle Finally Shows Up (Fashionably Late)

One day my baby sister called and told me she had a dream that my daughter started talking again. At that point, I was like "whatever" to any shred of hope. I had developed a protective skepticism thicker than Got2B Ultra Glued gel.

That evening, I was reading the Bible to my daughter—the book of Job, in case you're wondering, because apparently I have a flair for the dramatic. Job is what you read when you're in the pits but don't know any other option. It's like the original "things could always be worse" pep talk.

At this point, my girl would only have moments of lucidity very late at night or early in the morning. Those moments were precious—like getting to visit with her before she'd slip away again.

Well, this particular night as I was reading Job (seriously, not even one of the happy, encouraging parts), out of NOWHERE she started reading it with me. I froze, my brain unable to process what was happening. Apparently she was shocked too, because she immediately took off running like she'd seen a ghost.

I stood there, mouth hanging open, the Bible still in my hands. The words she had spoken hung in the air like magic. My daughter—my little girl who had been so lost to us—had found her voice again.

In that moment, all the prayers, all the tears, all the nights of questioning started to make sense. Not because I suddenly understood WHY any of this had happened, but because I witnessed firsthand what faith ultimately produces: perseverance that leads to breakthrough.

What I hadn't realized was that her brain was literally rebuilding itself. She had to start OVER. Imagine being born again at age nine. It was EXACTLY like that. As time progressed, she started to learn how to write again. Her elementary school teacher would come to the house and work with her—first seeing her write nothing more than circles and pointing to words, then writing her name, then speaking actual sentences.

Her favorite word was "waffle." Don't ask me why. That was her response to EVERYTHING. "How are you feeling?" "Waffle." "Do you want to try walking?" "Waffle." For a while there, I thought we might need to legally change her name to Waffle.

Her recovery was S-L-O-W. It was painful. It changed her. It changed ME.

The journey of watching her relearn everything—how to control her body, how to express herself, how to engage with the world—was both heartbreaking and awe-inspiring. There were setbacks. Days when it seemed like we'd lost ground. Moments of frustration so intense that I thought neither of us would survive them.

But there were also triumphs, small victories that accumulated over time like precious stones, forming a path back to wholeness. It was less like the dramatic movie scene where the patient suddenly wakes up completely healed, and more like watching a flower bloom in slow motion—beautiful in its gradual unfolding.

And let me tell you something about my miracle girl. As I write this, I'm watching an honest-to-goodness, eye-rolling, TikTok-dancing 18-year-old young woman bouncing around my house. EIGHTEEN! Can someone please explain how that happened? Wasn't I just changing diapers like... last Tuesday?

This kid—my goodness—she laughs so loud the neighbors probably think we're hosting a comedy club. She's constantly creating something, dreaming up big plans, and explaining TikTok trends to me that make absolutely zero sense. (And yes, I've tried to learn the dances. No, we will not be discussing the results. My dignity has suffered enough.)

But here's the thing that stops me in my tracks sometimes: she's ALIVE. Actually, gloriously, messily alive. And if you've followed our story on social media, you know that wasn't a given.

Because just when we thought we were done with medical drama—PLOT TWIST!—2022 rolled in with a pulmonary embolism. I swear, sometimes I think our family gets medical emergencies instead of birthday presents. Blood clots in her lungs, people! The doctors threw around terrifying words like "CTEPH" and "chronic pulmonary hypertension" while I nodded like I understood and then frantically Googled everything later in the hospital bathroom.

Two and a half weeks in the ICU, friends. Do you know what happens to a mother's under-eye bags after two weeks sleeping in a hospital chair? I looked like I was the patient.

But my girl? This warrior child? She bounced back, went back to school, and even ran track—ON PURPOSE! While taking enough daily medications to open a small pharmacy. For TWO YEARS.

Finally, after enough doctor visits to qualify for our own parking space, the cardiology team said those words: "We think she needs specialized surgery." Which is how Genesis and I ended up in San Diego, in yet another hospital, about to face yet another mountain.

I won't go deep into the surgery details (that's another book's worth of stress-eating and prayer journals), but imagine hearing that the best surgeon in the WORLD is going to remove blood clots from your child's body by cooling her body, putting it on ice, stopping all blood flow, and then taking a tool to scrape the remnants of blood clots from her tiny vessels. This surgeon removed eighteen blood clots from the right and left sides of her lungs. EIGHTEEN.

But here's the miracle: it worked. That incredible surgeon removed every single clot, and my baby is free. Free from that disease, free from those medications, free to write her own story now.

Sometimes I catch myself just watching her—dancing around her bedroom like nobody's watching, laughing so hard with her little sister, hunched over her iPad creating something beautiful at the kitchen table.

And in those moments? I can't breathe from the gratitude. My chest actually hurts with it. Because this—THIS is what faith looks like when it finally pays off. Not some perfect, pristine, Instagram-worthy moment. But a loud, messy, beautiful teenager who has no idea her mom is creepily watching her exist and silently ugly-crying with thankfulness.

Faith doesn't always show up in burning bushes, friends. Sometimes it shows up in medical discharge papers and teenage eye-rolls. And let me tell you—both are absolutely sacred.

What Faith REALLY Looks Like (Spoiler: It's Not Always Pretty)

What I've come to understand about faith is that there has to be something that activates it. Kind of like courage. Or those glow sticks you get at concerts—they don't do anything until you crack them. (Is that the most profound metaphor ever? No. But it's accurate.)

Faith isn't static. It's not a badge you wear or a certificate you frame and hang on the wall. It's dynamic, responsive, activated by challenge and adversity. It's EASY to say you have faith when everything's sunshine and rainbows. The true test—and the true growth—comes when you're asked to believe despite what your eyes see, despite what logic dictates, despite what fear whispers (or sometimes screams) in your ear.

Faith is like that friend who doesn't just show up for the party but stays to help clean up afterward when there's juice on the carpet and someone's kid threw up in your favorite houseplant. ANYONE can believe when things are awesome. The real faith muscles develop when everything's falling apart and you're standing in the metaphorical rubble wondering what hit you.

And here's something nobody tells you: faith isn't the absence of doubt. Some of the most faith-filled moments of my life have been absolutely RIDDLED with questions, with uncertainty, with the very human experience of wondering if I'm getting it all wrong. Faith doesn't eliminate these questions; it just gives us the courage to keep walking even as we ask them.

When Life Keeps Throwing Curveballs (And You Never Played Baseball)

When I first wrote this chapter, I was in yet ANOTHER life crisis. (Seriously, God? A little break would be nice.) I hadn't seen my oldest son in over two weeks because he was locked in a juvenile detention center. The morning of his arrest, I was told he would probably come home the following day.

Truth: He did not come home the following day.

Once again I found myself wondering what in the actual heck was going on. Why was this happening to me? Why did my grandmother have to pass away just a month prior? Why did my brother have to have a massive heart attack a month before THAT? Doesn't God understand I'm trying to write an inspirational book here? Doesn't He hear me when I ask Him to protect my family and bless my children? Haven't I gone through ENOUGH?

Have you ever had those moments where you feel like raising your hand and saying, "Excuse me, God? I think there's been a scheduling error. I already had my big life challenge this decade. This must be meant for someone else—perhaps that person who was rude to me at Target or the one who cut me off in the school drop-off lane?"

These questions pounded in my mind like a toddler with a wooden spoon on your best cookware. And I don't have answers—not satisfying ones, anyway. I can recite all the spiritual platitudes I've heard: "God doesn't give you more than you can handle." "Everything happens for a reason." "It's all part of God's plan."

But in the raw moments of grief and worry and frustration, these words feel about as helpful as a chocolate teapot. Sometimes I want to respond to those platitudes with, "Well, maybe God has SERIOUSLY overestimated me, because I am definitely not handling this well."

I'm just being honest because none of this makes sense. I've had to learn to say, "Not my will, but God's," even when God's will seems to be taking me through every difficult situation known to humankind.

You have NO IDEA how badly I wanted to storm that detention center and get my child. When I spoke with my son, I could not tell him when he would come home, and it broke me into a million tiny pieces. I'm not dismissing what led him there. I'm just expressing that I wanted nothing more than to have my children home where they belong, preferably in bubble wrap until they're 35.

The beautiful part of that story is that my son eventually overcame that darkest season of his life and is now living on his own, working, successful, and mentoring others. What a testimony! But here's what I didn't tell you—I did march up to that detention center and got my child... and things didn't magically get better. They seemed to get worse...until I surrendered.

And this is perhaps the most difficult aspect of faith—surrendering our will, our desires, our plans to something larger than ourselves. Not in a way that diminishes our agency or our legitimate feelings, but in a way that acknowledges that we don't see the whole picture. Our perspective is limited. There may be purposes at work that we cannot yet perceive.

Faith in someone or something doesn't equate to getting the outcome you want. I have faith in God and sometimes things still go to absolute crap. I believe in my children and they still occasionally make decisions that make me question whether they were raised by wolves. That is just LIFE.

This isn't the motivational poster version of faith with the sunset and the inspiring quote. This is the gritty, real-life version that sometimes includes curse words and ugly crying and questioning everything. But isn't that actually more authentic than a sanitized faith that never encounters doubt or disappointment?

Finding Faith in Unexpected Places (Like Weekly Phone Calls)

After my dad's mom passed away, I decided to reconnect with my mother's mom, my Grandma Hattie. I had never lost love for her—not at all. It's just that distance had kept us from being as close as we once were. I missed that connection.

So, I reached out, and now we talk every week. Wednesdays are our day, and our conversations always start the same way: "I'm blessed and highly favored." I get to enjoy an hour of her preaching to me and telling me about her week, and I LOVE it because I don't even get a chance to vent or complain. We start praying, and somehow all my problems shrink down to their proper size.

There's something about the ritual of it—the familiarity, the way her voice carries the weight of decades spent talking to God. It centers me, reminds me of what actually matters, connects me to something bigger than my immediate problems.

In those moments of prayer with my grandmother, I feel part of something ancient and ongoing—a current of belief that has sustained countless generations through their own trials and triumphs. It's like tapping into a power source that's been running long before I arrived and will continue long after I'm gone.

One morning after prayer, she was talking to me about love. About how difficult it is to love someone when they're acting like a complete jerk (ok, she used nicer words, but you get the idea). The devotional she was reading focused on how love disarms hate.

It's an easy concept to grasp intellectually. But let's be real—

when someone is hateful to me, my first instinct is not to love them back. It's to draft a strongly worded text message that I'll hopefully delete before sending.

That conversation made me think about other concepts that sound simple but are actually Mount Everest-level difficult.

Like forgiveness.

When Forgiveness Feels Impossible (But Necessary)

I remember when my husband and I were newly married. I was DETERMINED to make our blended family work. I was literally doing THE MOST. I made chore schedules with color coding. I conducted family meetings with actual agendas. I listened to advice from people who had absolutely no idea what they were talking about.

I was basically a blended family cruise director—overscheduling, overplanning, overthinking every interaction. If I had known Pinterest had existed back then, I would have been their poster child, complete with color-coded conflict resolution charts and themed family dinners.

Someone suggested we try family counseling. Which, honestly, is not a bad idea. I think more people should see a therapist—a good one, not one from a horror movie, which is foreshadowing for what's about to happen in this story.

I began searching for a therapist. Where to start? Church, of course. There were no services our church provided, but they referred us to a local Christian college. I made some calls and we landed on a provisionally licensed therapist who seemed nice. We connected right away.

Our first family session went well. Everyone got to speak, and we received some advice on managing conflicts. One "interesting" coping skill she suggested was to stop and sit down (regardless of location) and count to ten if a child was acting out.

Let me tell you something about our family—we are NOT sit-down-and-count-to-ten in Wal-Mart people. But okay. I was willing to try anything.

We set up individual sessions for the children, and our therapy journey began. One child after another visited with the new therapist. A few weeks in, our schedules got complicated. My husband was working long hours, I was juggling work and school for the kids, and oh yeah—I was pregnant. Because apparently running a blended family wasn't challenging enough.

One day my husband was late to a session. The therapist had some words for him about it. Now, one thing to know about my husband—he's a bit rough around the edges. He'll give it to you straight, no chaser. So when the therapist attempted to lecture him about being late, he basically told her to stay in her lane.

The following evening was our scheduled family session. We arrived and sat in the lobby as usual. The therapist came out, took our payment, and then asked if the children could go back with her while we waited in the lobby.

Sure, no problem. That seems normal. SPOILER: IT WAS NOT NORMAL.

After about thirty minutes, I started getting this feeling in the pit of my stomach. You know the one—that maternal instinct that something isn't right. My husband was getting antsy too. We waited longer. Eventually, I went to the counter and called out for assistance. No one appeared.

The minutes stretched into what felt like years as worry transformed into full-blown panic. All the worst possibilities raced through my mind—what was happening to my children? Were they scared? Did they need me?

An hour passed. NOTHING. So, I did the next best thing. I called my mama. She told me to call the police. I hung up and called the police. When I finally got someone on the line, they told me a cruiser was already headed to the facility.

Wait, what? Why would police already be on their way?

My heart dropped to my toes. I was now SCREAMING for my children. No response.

Another hour crawled by.

Finally, the therapist emerged from the back…with a police officer. My husband and I exchanged confused looks as we were instructed to enter a conference room. There sat our children around a table, looking confused and frightened.

Why? Because this therapist had accused us of ABUSE.

The officers interviewed each child while we sat there in shock. I stared at the therapist with such disbelief and hurt and utter rage that I'm surprised she didn't burst into flames. She KNEW how triggering this was for me because I had shared my own experiences with her.

After another hour of questioning, the officers found no reason to keep our children from us (surprise, surprise). They did, however, offer some threatening words before allowing us to take our traumatized family home.

In that moment, I felt violated in a way that's hard to put into words. This woman had taken our vulnerability—our willingness to seek help, our openness about our struggles, our trust in bringing our children to her—and weaponized it against us.

The betrayal cut deeper than a paper cut between your fingernail bed (and those things HURT). Not just because of what she'd done, but because of what it represented: the risk inherent in trusting others with our most precious treasures—our children and our truth. It was like opening your home to someone and having them rob you—except what they took was far more valuable than any possession.

One of our children mentioned feeling sad during the questioning, which resulted in him and my husband spending the night in the psychiatric ward for "observation." Because apparently being upset that someone falsely accused your family of abuse is a concerning reaction? Make it make sense.

The children were traumatized. They thought they were going to be taken from us. They later told us the therapist had been trying to pressure them into saying they were being abused.

The Hard Road to Forgiveness (Which Feels More Like a Mountain Climb)

I woke up the next morning with vengeance in my heart. The kind of rage that makes your vision go blurry around the edges. I wanted this woman to PAY. I wanted her license revoked. I wanted billboards with her face and "WORST THERAPIST EVER" in giant letters. I was beyond furious.

The rage was all-consuming. I fantasized about confronting her, exposing her, making sure she could never harm another family. My thoughts were dark, fueled by a toxic cocktail of maternal protectiveness, righteous anger, and raw hurt.

I couldn't eat. I couldn't sleep. I couldn't focus. I was like a mama bear whose cubs had been threatened, except instead of claws and teeth, I was considering lawsuits and licensing board complaints and possibly a strongly worded Yelp review.

I didn't want to do something I'd later regret, so I consulted my Pastor. I thought—hoped—he would give me permission to unleash holy vengeance. His response? An email with the "F" word in it.

No, not THAT F-word. The other one.

Forgive.

Are you KIDDING me? You want me to forgive the woman who tried to rip my new family apart? You want me to forgive the woman who traumatized my children and gave them trust issues they'll probably need therapy for? (The irony is not lost on me.) No way. Not a chance. Not happening.

I allowed that situation to sit in my heart like an unwelcome houseguest.

For years.

I looked her up periodically, checking to see if she was still practicing. Each time her name would appear, I would remember what she did, and the rage would flare up fresh and hot.

This unforgiveness became part of my identity—this righteous anger, this justified resentment. It was like a stone I carried, taking it out occasionally to examine, to feel its weight, to remind myself of the injury that had been done.

And in doing so, I kept the wound fresh. I prevented it from healing. I allowed it to define a part of my story. It became my personal pet grudge—I fed it, nurtured it, kept it alive long after other memories had faded.

I've heard people say "forgiveness is not for the other person, it's for you." That sounds so cute, doesn't it? Like something you'd find cross-stitched on a pillow or something. I couldn't see how this situation and my unforgiveness was impacting my life. I felt like my only piece of revenge was to hate this woman with the fire of a thousand suns.

However, I noticed I couldn't tell that story without my blood pressure shooting through the roof.

Meanwhile, this woman went on with her life. Completely unbothered. She never apologized or reached out. We had zero closure.

It wasn't until I was in the middle of my daughter's illness, crying out to God for healing, that my heart was reminded of this grudge. I didn't want ANYTHING holding me back from receiving a miracle. No grudge. No unforgiveness. No bitterness. NOTHING.

I had to release my grip on that old wound. I decided to forgive her and anyone else I felt wronged me. I wrote their names down (it was a LONG list, people), and I simply said, "I forgive."

The Day-by-Day Work of Faith (AKA The Never-Ending Construction Project)

The hurt didn't magically disappear. It still stings sometimes. Sometimes I have to say "I forgive" all over again when I allow myself to get angry about what happened.

Forgiveness isn't a one-and-done kind of thing. It's the most difficult thing to do when the person who hurt you isn't even sorry. It's easy to forgive someone who apologizes sincerely. How about that person who cuts you off in traffic and then holds up their hand to signal they're sorry? It completely diffuses the road rage, doesn't it?

But play that scenario again and imagine the hand gesture is a middle finger. Forgive? That's HARD. It's like your brain immediately starts drafting an angry letter to God about the audacity of some people.

And here we see the connection between faith and

forgiveness—both require us to move beyond what we can see, beyond what makes logical sense. Both ask us to embrace a reality that transcends our immediate circumstances. Both demand a kind of surrender that goes against every self-protective instinct we have.

This is why faith and forgiveness are often mentioned together in spiritual traditions. They're cut from the same cloth, woven from the same thread. They both ask us to live as if there's more to reality than what we can see with our limited vision, more to the story than what we currently know, more possibility than what seems available in any given moment.

I'm learning that the most powerful tool is to extend love and forgiveness especially when you don't want to. ESPECIALLY when the other person doesn't deserve it. ESPECIALLY when every cell in your body is screaming for justice instead of mercy.

And isn't this the essence of faith? To act in accordance with what we believe to be true, even when—ESPECIALLY when—it runs counter to our natural inclinations. To choose love when hate seems more satisfying. To offer grace when judgment feels more justified. To remain open to possibility when cynicism appears more realistic.

Faith, at its core, is not about being certain. It's about being willing. Willing to see beyond the immediate dumpster fire you might be experiencing. Willing to trust in what we cannot fully understand. Willing to keep moving forward even when the path ahead looks like it's covered in LEGO bricks and you're barefoot.

And in that willingness, we discover capacities for resilience, growth, and transformation that we never knew we possessed.

So I continue to walk this path of faith—stumbling frequently, questioning constantly, but always moving forward. Because I've seen what faith can produce, not just in dramatic moments of healing or breakthrough, but in ordinary moments of choosing love over hate, hope over despair, possibility over limitation.

And in those choices, made day after day (sometimes minute by minute), I find myself becoming more fully who I was created to be. Not perfect, not without questions, but authentically on this journey—with all its detours, potholes, and unexpected vistas—that is uniquely mine.

The Woman in the Mirror

Let's talk about that moment when someone else sees you completely differently than you see yourself. There I was, minding my own business in the kitchen—you know, that sacred space where I can actually hear my own thoughts for five seconds—when I heard it.

"MOM!"

"WHAT?!" (This wasn't so much a question as it was the universal parental sound of being startled out of a peaceful moment.)

"You're famous!"

Wait, what? Famous? Me? Excuse me while I laugh into my coffee mug.

My daughter had spotted me on the local news. A tiny little segment that lasted maybe three minutes. To her, this was basically the equivalent of me walking the red carpet at the Oscars. In her eyes, I was FAMOUS with all capital letters.

But you know what immediately happened in my brain? The Impostor Monster woke up, stretched, and said, "Well, hello there! Time to remind you that you don't belong in the spotlight!"

Isn't it fascinating how our children see us so differently than we see ourselves? In my daughter's eyes, I was this incredible, accomplished woman worthy of admiration and awe. But there I stood, feeling that uncomfortable tightness in my chest, wondering if viewers were judging me, questioning why I was even on their TV screens, waiting for someone to point at me and shout, "FRAUD!"

The irony is that there was no fraud happening. I was simply being myself—sharing knowledge I actually had, talking about experiences I'd genuinely lived. Yet the Impostor Monster insisted otherwise.

The Award Nomination That Nearly Broke Me
Speaking of feeling like a fraud, let me tell you about the time I was nominated for an award. Not just any award—one that only 10 people in my entire city receive each year.

When that email notification popped up in my inbox, I legitimately read it THREE TIMES before it registered in my brain. My first thought wasn't excitement or pride. It was, "They must have the wrong email address." I literally checked to make sure they had spelled my name correctly.

Once I confirmed it was actually meant for me (yes, they did know who they were nominating), the next wave hit: "What if I go through this whole process and they realize I'm actually the LEAST accomplished person they've ever considered? What if my application is so pathetic they create a new category just for me called 'Most Delusional Applicant'?"

These fears nearly stopped me from even completing the application. I'm not exaggerating. I almost deleted the email and pretended it never happened. The application required detailed descriptions of my contributions, innovations, and impact. Each question might as well have said, "Please brag about yourself here." And let me tell you—for someone raised the way I was, this felt like being asked to run naked through a shopping mall. THE DISCOMFORT WAS REAL.

I would type a sentence about something I'd accomplished, then immediately feel this overwhelming urge to add, "But it wasn't really that big a deal" or "Anyone could have done it." Writing even the most objectively true statements about my work felt like I was claiming to have invented electricity or cured cancer.

Growing up in a religious household, I was taught that any talents or gifts came from God. If you had any natural abilities that brought you recognition, they weren't actually YOURS—they were on loan from the Almighty. That meant seeking awards or accolades was basically spiritual selfishness. Owning your greatness? That's called PRIDE, honey, and it comes before a fall.

My mother constantly quoted the Bible: "Let someone else praise you, not your own mouth." Great advice for not being an insufferable braggart at dinner parties, but TERRIBLE preparation for filling out an award application that literally asks you to list your accomplishments.

The line between humility and self-erasure had become so blurred that I couldn't even accurately represent my achievements when EXPLICITLY ASKED for them. It's like I'd developed an allergic reaction to acknowledging my own efforts.

Interestingly, I'd been nominated for this same award the year before and hadn't made it past the first round. At the time, I assumed it was because I wasn't "worthy" enough. It never occurred to me that maybe—just maybe—I hadn't effectively communicated my accomplishments because I was too busy downplaying them.

But something had shifted since that first nomination. Maybe it was seeing the tangible impact of my work with women and girls. Maybe it was the persistent encouragement from mentors who kept insisting I take ownership of my contributions. Whatever the reason, I decided to step into the discomfort this time.

The application process became this unexpected journey of self-discovery. Each question forced me to reflect on what I had ACTUALLY accomplished, what challenges I had GENUINELY overcome, what impact my work had TRULY created. Slowly, reluctantly, I began to see the pattern of contribution that others had already recognized in me.

The Monster of Self-Doubt (And Why It's So Darn Persistent)

Impostor syndrome can rob you of your greatest moments because you're too busy waiting for someone to stand up and shout, "SHE DOESN'T BELONG HERE!" You spend so much mental energy worrying about being "found out" that you can't even enjoy or fully participate in the experience happening right in front of you.

For me, the Impostor Monster constantly whispers things like: "They're gonna know, you aren't as worthy as everyone thought." "Anyone could have done what you did." "They only chose you because [insert real person who deserved it more] wasn't available." "If they knew the REAL you, they'd never have selected you."

But here's the truth bomb I had to eventually face: These thoughts couldn't be further from reality.

The journey to where I am today wasn't lined with lucky breaks and happy accidents. It was HARD. There were sleepless nights juggling multiple responsibilities. Financial sacrifices that meant saying no to things I wanted so I could invest in things I needed. Relationships that couldn't withstand the demands of my commitments. Moments of doubt when I questioned if I was on the right path, if the work was making any difference, if it was all worth it.

But with each obstacle came growth. With each setback came learning. With each challenge came a deeper understanding of my own capacity and resilience.

I discovered strengths I didn't know I possessed—an ability to connect with people from wildly different backgrounds, a talent for making complex ideas accessible, a weird knack for bringing people together who would normally never interact.

These weren't magical gifts bestowed upon me while I slept. They were capabilities I developed through practice, through failure, through getting back up after falling flat on my face. Yes, maybe there were some natural tendencies—call them God-given—but they had been cultivated through disciplined work and conscious choice.

Yet even knowing all this, when I have to put those things on display, the fear still rises up. "You're not worthy; you just got lucky" creeps in like that one guy I dated who ate all my hotdogs and snacks and left wet towels on the bathroom floor.

But here's a perspective shift that changed everything for me: What if impostor syndrome isn't something to be eliminated but something to be embraced as a sign of growth?

I've come to see impostor syndrome not as an enemy to be vanquished but as a companion on the journey—an uncomfortable companion who snores loudly and takes up too much space, perhaps, but one that serves a purpose. When those feelings arise, they signal that I'm stretching beyond my comfort zone, that I'm taking on challenges that matter, that I'm continuing to grow rather than settling into complacency.

The most accomplished people I know—bestselling authors, business leaders, activists, artists—almost ALL confess to experiencing moments of doubt, moments when they question whether they deserve their success or worry about being "found out." Rather than being a sign of weakness, these feelings often indicate self-awareness and intellectual honesty.

Strategies for Overcoming (Or At Least Managing) the Monster

I've achieved real success despite the Impostor Monster riding shotgun, and I'm determined to keep moving forward regardless of its loud opinions. Nothing is stopping me. By pressing into success even when I feel like a fraud, I've developed coping mechanisms that actually work—not just for me, but potentially for you too.

My favorite? The *"Yep, I Did That"* file.

This is a LITERAL folder (both physical and digital) that documents things I've accomplished, lives I've impacted, awards I've received, degrees I've earned. Why? Because I DID THAT. I was strong enough to do that. And—dare I say it—I did a damn good job.

I didn't break down and give up when challenges came. I did it. All of it.

My "Yep I Did That" file started as a simple manila folder where I kept thank-you notes and certificates. Over time, it evolved into a dedicated drawer in my filing cabinet filled with evidence of impact and achievement. There's the letter from a young woman who participated in one of my first workshops, who wrote years later to tell me how that experience had changed the trajectory of her life. The program from the conference where I gave my first keynote address, despite being so terrified I nearly threw up backstage. The newspaper clipping about the community initiative that grew from a small idea into a program that's still running today.

This file serves multiple purposes. On those days when self-doubt is screaming through a megaphone, it provides concrete reminders of capability and contribution. When preparing for new challenges, it offers perspective on how far I've come and how much I've already overcome. When mentoring others struggling with their own inadequacy feelings, it demonstrates the value of acknowledging achievement instead of dismissing it.

Building this file required overcoming the discomfort of saving evidence of success. My initial instinct was to quickly file away or even trash recognition—as if keeping it might be seen as vain or self-important. But I've learned that honoring achievement isn't the same as inflating it. Acknowledging real impact isn't the same as exaggerating it.

So when those moments creep up saying, "They're going to find you out," "They're going to see right through you," "You're going to be exposed as a fraud," I can flip through my file and say, "I EARNED this. I WORKED for this. I DID this."

Another strategy I've developed is intentionally reframing how I think about expertise. I used to believe that to speak on a topic, I needed to know EVERYTHING about it—to have mastered every nuance, read every publication, anticipated every possible question. This impossible standard guaranteed feelings of inadequacy, no matter how much knowledge I actually possessed.

Now I understand that expertise exists on a spectrum.

Being a valuable contributor doesn't require being the world's foremost authority; it requires having something worthwhile to offer based on experience, study, or perspective. I don't need to know everything to have earned the right to speak about something. I can acknowledge the limitations of my knowledge while still confidently sharing what I DO know.

I've also learned to distinguish between normal nervousness about stretching into new territory and the more insidious voice of the Impostor Monster. The former is natural and can actually enhance performance by keeping me alert and engaged. The latter only seeks to undermine and diminish, to keep me small and safe at the expense of making an impact.

Inherent Worth (The Game-Changing Realization)

I want to take a moment and reflect on the fact that I am deserving. I want to acknowledge that I didn't force this. My worthiness isn't predicated upon how many awards I have. It's not determined by how many letters come after my name. It doesn't depend on how many children I've raised or degrees I've earned. It's not based on my bank account balance or who I know in high places.

I was worthy the moment I came into this world. I was deserving from my first breath. Which means I can enter any space confidently, stand flat-footed, and declare that I am worthy.

I am deserving!

This realization—that worth is inherent rather than earned—represents the most profound shift in my thinking. For SO LONG, I operated as if worthiness were a status to achieve through accumulation: accumulation of credentials, accomplishments, recognition, relationships. I treated it as conditional, provisional, always potentially revocable if I failed to maintain certain standards or meet certain expectations.

The exhaustion of this approach eventually became unsustainable. No amount of external validation could fill the internal void created by the belief that I was fundamentally unworthy unless proven otherwise. And no achievement was ever enough to silence the voice that said, "Yes, but what have you done LATELY?"

The alternative perspective—that worthiness is an intrinsic quality of being human—didn't come easily. It required unlearning deeply ingrained beliefs about value and deservingness. It meant questioning cultural messages about productivity and success. It involved recognizing how systems of oppression had shaped my understanding of who matters and why.

This shift didn't happen overnight. It began with small experiments in self-acceptance, moments of treating myself with the same compassion I would offer a dear friend. It grew through practices of mindfulness that allowed me to observe self-critical thoughts without automatically believing them. It deepened through relationships with people who modeled a different way of being—people who seemed to understand instinctively that their value wasn't tied to their output.

Gradually, I came to see that worthiness isn't something to be earned but something to be recognized and remembered. It's the foundation upon which achievement is built, not the result of it. When I operate from this understanding, I'm often MORE productive, MORE creative, MORE impactful—because I'm no longer draining energy into proving my right to exist or contribute.

Writing Through Fear (The Ultimate Irony)

Let me share the most ridiculous example of my impostor syndrome: I started writing a book about impostor syndrome... and then abandoned it because of MY OWN impostor syndrome.

I'm not even kidding. I couldn't make this up if I tried.

After developing an outline, completing initial research, and drafting several chapters, I found myself absolutely paralyzed by doubt. Who was I to write authoritatively about this topic? What if psychology professionals criticized my approach? What if readers found nothing new or helpful in my perspective?

These questions loomed larger each time I sat down to write, until eventually I just... stopped sitting down. The manuscript gathered digital dust on my hard drive. The notes and interviews collected were filed away. I redirected my energy toward "safer" projects that felt less exposing.

But that abandoned book HAUNTED me. It represented a conversation I'd wanted to have, a contribution I'd believed was important. In quiet moments, I would remember the people who had shared their stories with me during the research phase—people who had trusted me with their vulnerabilities, who had expressed enthusiasm about the project's potential to help others. I had let them down, and I had let myself down.

The turning point came unexpectedly. During a conversation with a young woman I was mentoring, she confessed to feeling like a fraud in her new leadership role. As I shared some of my own experiences with impostor syndrome, she asked if I could recommend any books on the topic.

When I mentioned I had actually started writing one but shelved it because I "wasn't qualified enough," the absurdity of the situation suddenly hit me like a water balloon on a hot day. There I was, perpetuating the very cycle I had hoped to help others break. Talk about practicing what you DON'T preach!

That conversation catalyzed a period of deep reflection on what was really holding me back. It wasn't lack of qualification—I had both the research and lived experience to make a meaningful contribution. It wasn't concern for academic rigor—I had been thorough in my approach.

No, what held me back was fear—fear of being seen, of being judged, of making myself vulnerable by putting my thoughts into the world where they could be criticized or dismissed. And underlying that fear was the persistent belief that my voice didn't matter enough to be heard, that my insights weren't valuable enough to be shared.

I began talking to that girl in the mirror. "You are worthy! Your words matter. The achievements you've attained? No one else did those for you. The impact you've made in others' lives isn't exaggerated."

That conversation with the mirror became a daily practice. Sometimes it was affirmative: "You have something worth saying. Your perspective matters." Sometimes it was challenging: "What's the worst that could happen if someone disagrees with what you write? Can you survive a negative review?" Sometimes it was simply compassionate: "You're trying something difficult. It's okay to be scared. Write scared."

Gradually, the practice began to shift something fundamental. The woman behind the curtain—the authentic self I had been hiding from the world out of fear of judgment or rejection—began to emerge. She was imperfect but insightful, uncertain at times but deeply committed to growth, still learning but already knowledgeable.

She was, in short, exactly the person who should be writing a book about navigating impostor syndrome—not because she had conquered it completely, but because she understood intimately its terrain and had developed practical strategies for traversing it.

A Message of Empowerment (Not Just for Me, but for YOU)

You need to remind yourself too. YOU did that. YOU got that promotion. YOU earned that raise because you deserved it, because you worked hard for it. YOU landed that dream job because you were qualified for it. YOU won that award because somebody recognized your greatness. YOU created that change that has improved lives. YOU spoke up for the defenseless when no one else would because you were strong enough, bold enough.

You deserve any and all accolades that come your way. You ARE all the great things you believe you are on your best days. You ARE that mind-blowingly smart, capable, creative person.

This message isn't just for me; it's for anyone who has ever questioned their right to take up space, to use their voice, to receive recognition. It's for the woman who hesitates to apply for a promotion because she's not sure she checks EVERY box in the job description, despite consistently exceeding expectations in her current role. It's for the man who downplays his contributions to a successful project, attributing the outcome to luck rather than acknowledging his critical role.

It's for the first-generation college student who feels out of place among peers with more privileged backgrounds, who works twice as hard but still wonders if they truly belong. It's for the person from a marginalized community who has been made to feel that their presence in certain spaces is conditional, dependent on performing perfectly and never making mistakes.

It's for everyone who has ever received positive feedback and immediately discounted it, who has achieved something significant and immediately moved the goalposts, who has received an opportunity and immediately questioned whether they deserve it.

What if we collectively decided to take ownership of our capabilities, to acknowledge our growth, to celebrate our contributions? What if we recognized that doing so isn't arrogant but accurate, isn't boastful but honest? What if we understood that false modesty doesn't serve anyone—not ourselves, not those who might be inspired by our example, not those who benefit from our fully expressed gifts?

Imagine the energy that would be liberated if we weren't constantly questioning our worthiness. Imagine the creative potential that would be unleashed if we weren't constantly undermining our own authority. Imagine the impact that would be possible if we allowed ourselves to operate from a place of confidence rather than doubt.

The woman in the mirror doesn't need to hide anymore. She has always been worthy. She has always had something valuable to offer.

And so have you.

The Art of Truly Hearing

I'm gonna get really real for a minute. You know how some people are naturally gifted at singing or can pick up any sport like they've been doing it their whole life? Well, I have a special talent too—but it's not one you'll find on any resume or talent show. My superpower is hearing one thing and somehow transforming it into something COMPLETELY different.

I'm like a verbal processing magician, except I'm usually the one most surprised by what comes out of the hat.

This quirky little processing glitch has been with me since forever. And it's not that I don't pay attention—I swear I do! It's not that I don't care about what people are saying—I care deeply! It's more like there's this rogue translation service operating between my ears and my brain, and sometimes that service takes some WILD creative liberties with the content.

Picture having your own personal dubbing team working inside your head, except they're understaffed, running on too much caffeine and not enough sleep, and occasionally just making things up because they missed the deadline. That's my daily reality, friends.

Has this little quirk caused some awkward moments in my life? OH MY GOODNESS, YES. Has it created confusion, embarrassment, and even conflict in my relationships? Absolutely. But has it also created some of the most hilarious moments that have my family still laughing years later? You bet it has.

This isn't something I chose, but it's definitely shaped how I navigate conversations, how I connect with others, and ultimately, how I've had to develop some serious strategies to make sure I'm actually hearing what people are saying and not what my creative brain wants to believe they're saying.

The Birth of the Fraggles Theory

Picture this: I'm five years old, and my favorite guy in the whole world—my daddy—is dropping me off at school. We pull up in his Oldsmobile, and I eagerly hop out, excited for the day ahead. As I'm running toward the school building, I hear my dad roll down the window and call out: "Have a good day, Rae-Rae!"

I stop, turn around, and look back. Now, at this point, the little information processors in my head (which my five-year-old imagination had decided were tiny Fraggles living in my ears) have just received a message. They think they've got it, but they're not entirely sure. So they ask me to check.

"What?" I yell back in my best five-year-old country drawl.

My dad yells again: "Have a good day, Rae-Rae!"

This time the Fraggles think they've nailed it.

Let me pause here and confess that my imagination has ALWAYS been off the charts. I believed in every childhood fantasy that came on television with my whole heart. In my little mind, I had decided that Fraggles were tiny fuzzy creatures living in my ears, and their job was to help me hear messages people were saying. Was this true? Obviously not.

But to a five-year-old who was the only one who knew about this theory—who was going to tell me I was wrong?

So the Fraggles have delivered their translation, and what did they tell me? They informed me that my father was speaking in an Australian accent and had used a cool new word I'd never heard before. It was obviously a new way of saying goodbye, and honestly, I was INTO IT.

With a big gummy smile, I lift up my hand to wave and yell back: "AVAGADANG TO YOU TOO, MATE!"

Because Australians say "mate," right? I was quite sure of this critical fact because I'd watched Crocodile Dundee. (Well, the parts my parents let me see, anyway.)

My poor dad. He didn't have the heart to correct me. He just smiled that smile parents give when they're witnessing something both ridiculous and precious happening simultaneously. He waved and drove away while I strutted into the schoolhouse, secretly thrilled with my new Australian vocabulary word.

I can still picture the look on my father's face—that beautiful mixture of confusion, amusement, and that special tenderness parents save for their children's most adorable mistakes. He could have corrected me, pulled me back to the car, and explained that he'd simply wished me a good day. But something in his parental wisdom told him to let this one ride, to allow me the joy of believing I'd discovered something exotic and new.

Throughout that day, I tried out my new phrase on several classmates, who looked at me with those perfectly confused kindergarten expressions. "Avagadang, mate!" I'd announce proudly, possibly with my version of an Australian accent that probably sounded more like a confused cowboy. Their blank stares didn't discourage me one bit—clearly they just weren't as worldly and sophisticated as I was.

By afternoon, I'd mostly forgotten about my linguistic discovery, but that moment stayed lodged in my father's memory. Years later, he would occasionally greet me with "Avagadang, mate!" and we would both dissolve into laughter at our private joke.

When Misinterpretation Leads to Public Embarrassment

Now, I know full well there aren't actually Fraggles living in my ears (disappointing, I know), but to this day, I still process things differently sometimes. And let me tell you about the time this tendency led to possibly the most mortifying job interview of my ENTIRE LIFE.

I applied for a position as a "Donor Specialist." I used to work at a tech firm that developed software for donor management, and through that experience, I'd heard stories from doctors and nurses about the organ transplant process. So when I saw "donor" in the job title, my brain immediately connected it to organ donation.

The thing is, I'd never actually worked directly with donor families or in organ procurement. My experience was entirely on the software side, helping organizations manage their donor information. But somehow, my brain decided this job must be about organ donation rather than what it actually was—working with people who make financial contributions to organizations.

I went into this interview COMPLETELY confident about my qualifications and experience. The only problem? The hiring manager obviously had a very different kind of donor in mind.

Y'all. I sat through almost the ENTIRE interview talking about donor management software and organ donation while they were asking about fundraising.

I kept wondering why they looked so confused when I mentioned my experience with the software system and referenced stories I'd heard about kidney or heart donors. The truly amazing (or horrifying, depending on your perspective) thing is they let me go through that entire interview without correcting me. It wasn't until the very end that the light bulb finally went off, leaving me with a feeling of humiliation that I still feel in my bones when I think about it.

The interview had started so promisingly! I arrived early, dressed in my most professional outfit, resume neatly organized in a leather portfolio. The receptionist was lovely, and the hiring manager's handshake was confident and warm. We exchanged pleasantries as she led me to a small conference room with a nice view of a courtyard.

"So," she began, "tell me about your experience with donor relations."

I launched into what I thought was an impressive narrative about my work with the donor management software, how it helped organizations track important information, and mentioned some of the stories I'd heard about the organ donation process from healthcare professionals. I talked about the technical aspects of the system and how it interfaced with hospital databases.

About five minutes into my enthusiastic response, I noticed a subtle shift in the hiring manager's expression. Her smile stayed fixed in place, but her eyes revealed growing confusion. She glanced down at my resume, then back at me, but didn't interrupt. Instead, she nodded and asked another question:

"And how would you approach cultivating relationships with potential major donors?"

This struck me as an odd question—software doesn't really "cultivate" relationships, and approaching hospitals about organ donation seemed like strange terminology. Still, I adapted my answer to focus on building trust with organizational partners and healthcare systems.

The interview continued this way for nearly THIRTY MINUTES. Each question seemed slightly off-topic from my perspective, but I figured maybe they used different terminology or perhaps had a new approach to donor coordination I hadn't encountered before.

It wasn't until the hiring manager asked about my experience with fundraising events that the pieces finally clicked into place. I felt a wave of heat rise from my neck to my face as understanding dawned. We had been having completely different conversations for the entire interview.

"I'm so sorry," I stammered, "but I think there's been a misunderstanding. I thought this position was related to organ donation management, not financial contributions."

The hiring manager's eyes widened slightly before she let out a small laugh. "Oh! That explains… well, quite a lot, actually."

We both laughed, but inside I was DYING. Not only had I completely misinterpreted the job description, but I had also spent half an hour confidently answering questions about a position I had zero experience for. The worst part wasn't even the embarrassment—it was knowing that I had wasted both our time because I hadn't clarified the meaning of a term I thought I understood.

I wanted to disappear into the carpet or perhaps claim

temporary insanity. Instead, I managed to maintain some semblance of professionalism while inwardly contemplating whether I could change my name and move to another state. To this day, I can't drive past that building without feeling my face flush all over again.

My Life-Saving Active Listening Toolkit

After years of miscommunications ranging from hilarious to heartbreaking, I've developed what I call my Active Listening Toolkit. These aren't just strategies I use—they're SURVIVAL SKILLS for someone whose brain occasionally decides to remix conversations like a DJ at a dance club.

Step 1: Actually Listen (Revolutionary, I Know)

The first step sounds ridiculously simple, but it's game-changing: ACTUALLY LISTEN to what is being said.

This means removing as many distractions as possible. Sometimes this isn't ideal, especially when your life is like mine. If there are no distractions in my house, something is probably wrong or about to go wrong. But I can eliminate the distractions that I control—putting my phone down when someone is talking, turning off the TV or music, relocating to a quieter space.

All of these actions are necessary for me to hear clearly what's being said. I'm a huge advocate of multi-tasking in life (hello, folding laundry while on conference calls!), but listening is one thing that I've had to accept requires my full attention.

My husband knows I struggle sometimes and he'll often say, "Look at me" when he needs to make sure I'm getting his message. There's something about that eye contact that helps both of us—it lets him know I'm focused, and it helps me stay anchored to what he's actually saying instead of what my brain might be creatively reimagining.

Because there's a massive difference between hearing and listening. My children will often call my name and ask me something when I'm working or otherwise engaged, and it takes them several attempts to get my attention. It's not because I don't hear them—I absolutely do. But I'm not listening.

My mother used to do the same thing to me and my siblings. "Mama, can we go outside?" would chime like a notification sound from a phone. Somewhere around the tenth repetition, my mom would yell, "I SAID YES!" And she most certainly had not audibly said that, or we would have been outside playing ages ago.

Creating an environment that supports active listening has become a crucial practice for me. In my business meetings with clients, this means taking notes during our conversations—not just to record what was said but to force my brain to process information in multiple ways simultaneously (hearing, understanding, writing). The act of writing helps anchor the information, preventing it from being transformed by my internal "translation service."

I've also found that physical positioning matters tremendously. Sitting directly across from someone, maintaining eye contact, and occasionally nodding not only signals to them that I'm engaged but also helps me stay focused on their words. The visual cues of lip movements and facial expressions provide additional context that helps my brain correctly interpret what I'm hearing.

Perhaps most importantly, I've learned to recognize the

situations where misinterpretation is most likely to occur. When I'm tired, stressed, or in environments with multiple conversations happening, my ability to accurately process information decreases significantly. In these situations, I'm more vigilant about employing all my active listening strategies.

Step 2: The Echo Technique (Not the Dr. Phil Way)

The second tool in my kit sounds simple but works magic: I repeat what I've been told.

This helps both me and the person who's speaking. Why? Avagadang, people. Need I say more?

There are times when what I've heard is NOT what has been said. At all. And before I plan actions based on what I think I was told, I need to repeat it for clarification.

I know it's important that I understand what the other person is saying so I can respond the correct way. So first, I try to comprehend what they're saying for both our sakes. Then I try to understand because I need to give them the right response. That's why I repeat what they said back to them.

And it's not the condescending kind of repetition like "What I think I heard you say is…" I cannot STAND when people do that. It's like a therapy move straight out of a self-help seminar. I just simply say what I heard and ask if that's right.

Dr. Phil does that "What I think you said…" thing, and it is SO annoying. But nonetheless, repeating information has proven incredibly successful for me.

The technique of repeating information has become second nature, particularly in my business. When a client outlines what they need from me, I'll often summarize the key points: "So you need this project completed by Friday, focusing on these specific elements, with particular attention to these details. Is that right?"

This approach serves multiple purposes—it confirms my understanding, shows I'm engaged with what they're saying, and gives me an opportunity for them to correct any misunderstandings before they lead to errors or wasted time. It's also saved me countless hours of working on the wrong thing or meeting the wrong expectations.

I've found that most people appreciate this approach rather than finding it annoying or redundant. In fact, many have commented that they wish more people would summarize conversations this way, as it often reveals assumptions or unspoken expectations that might otherwise go unaddressed.

The difference between my approach and the therapy-style "What I think I heard you say is…" lies in both intention and tone. I'm not trying to analyze or interpret emotional subtext; I'm simply confirming factual information to ensure we're on the same page. My repetition isn't performed with a knowing nod and sympathetic expression—it's straightforward, practical, and focused on clarity.

And it's especially easier when I try not to interrupt except when I need to repeat what they said. I make an effort to wait and talk only when they're done speaking. That way, I have enough time to process what they're saying.

Step 3: Embrace the "Stupid" Questions

The third essential tool in my kit: Get understanding even if you have to ask the "stupid" questions.

Now, I know we're supposed to say there are no dumb questions or stupid questions, but I come from a different school of thought. The stupid questions ARE the ones that don't need to be asked because the answers are right there in front of you. But, just because they're stupid, doesn't mean you shouldn't ask them anyway.

When I practice active listening, understanding is key. Had I asked a little more about that Donor Relations Specialist position, I would have known it was related to fundraising and not organ donation. And while that may have been an obvious question for those already familiar with the role, it was necessary for ME to understand, even at the risk of sounding uninformed.

Learning to ask clarifying questions has been one of the most valuable communication skills I've developed, but also one of the most difficult to implement consistently. There's a vulnerability in admitting you don't understand something, especially in professional settings where expertise is valued and assumptions of knowledge are everywhere.

The fear of appearing uninformed or unintelligent can be powerful, often leading us to nod along as if we comprehend perfectly, only to find ourselves confused or making errors later. It's like when someone mentions a book or movie everyone seems to know, and you nod enthusiastically rather than admit you've never heard of it. (I've definitely done the "Oh yeah, loved that one!" head nod about books I've never read. We all have.)

What I've come to realize is that the momentary discomfort of asking a clarifying question is FAR less painful than the potential consequences of proceeding with a misunderstanding. The embarrassment of that donor specialist interview could have been avoided with a simple question at the beginning: "Could you clarify what type of donors this position works with?"

So, whenever I'm in a networking event or mastermind group and someone uses terminology I'm not familiar with, I ask what they mean. Sometimes even if I know what it means, I ask anyway because there might be someone else in the room who has no idea what those initials stand for. Or if you're like me, you have a completely different understanding of what it means.

Someone else may be afraid to ask because they don't want to sound uninformed. So I help them out by asking myself. My philosophy is that no one should have to Google search terminology during a conversation just to understand what's being discussed. If I don't know something, I'm going to get clarity before we move on.

This willingness to ask questions has unexpectedly positioned me as an advocate for clarity in various settings. Other business owners have thanked me for asking about terms or industry jargon they didn't understand but were hesitant to question. In group settings, my requests for clarification often lead to more comprehensive explanations that benefit everyone present, not just me.

What began as a personal strategy to compensate for my processing quirk has evolved into a quality that promotes inclusivity and thorough understanding. By modeling the vulnerability required to ask questions, I create space for others to do the same, ultimately leading to better-informed decisions and fewer misunderstandings for everyone involved.

The irony isn't lost on me—my potential weakness in processing information has led me to develop a strength in facilitating clearer communication for entire groups. Sometimes our greatest challenges can become our most valuable contributions.

Step 4: Silence the Committee in Your Head

The final tool in my kit is perhaps the most challenging: shutting down the dialogues happening in my head while someone else is speaking.

Now that I'm certain Fraggles don't exist in my ears (disappointing, I know), I still do have an active and vivid imagination. Those inner distractions need to be silenced when someone is speaking to me so I can actually hear what they're saying.

I've learned to shut down my internal dialogue whenever someone else is speaking. If I had understood this as a child, I probably would have made those imaginary Fraggles be silent. That way, I would have clearly heard my dad say "Have a good day Rae-Rae" instead of "Avagadang."

The internal dialogue that runs through my mind during conversations can be DEAFENING if left unchecked. While someone is speaking, my brain might be simultaneously processing their words, planning my response, making associations with related topics, remembering similar conversations from the past, and noting environmental details like the speaker's tone or body language.

It's like having a committee meeting in my head while trying to listen to someone else—one voice is taking notes, another is planning what to say next, a third is remembering that I need to pick up milk on the way home, and a fourth is wondering if the speaker realizes they have a piece of spinach in their teeth.

This cognitive multitasking, while impressive in some ways, often interferes with accurate comprehension. Learning to quiet this mental chatter has been a practice requiring conscious effort and regular reinforcement. I've found that brief mindfulness techniques can help—taking a deep breath before an important conversation, deliberately focusing on the speaker's face, or mentally repeating their words as they say them to anchor my attention.

When I notice my mind wandering during a client call—perhaps planning my next Instagram post while they're explaining their project needs—I gently redirect my focus without self-criticism. This self-awareness has improved over time, allowing me to catch distractions earlier and return to attentive listening more quickly.

The practice of quieting my internal dialogue extends beyond just compensating for my processing quirk. It has enhanced my overall presence in conversations and relationships. Friends and family have commented that I seem more engaged, more responsive to nuances in conversation. In my business, it has improved my ability to truly understand what clients need without relying exclusively on written briefs or emails.

Embracing My Quirky Hearing as a Superpower

My journey with this processing quirk has been one of frustration, humor, adaptation, and ultimately acceptance. The misunderstandings it has caused have sometimes been embarrassing, occasionally hurtful, but also frequently hilarious. They have become part of my story, anecdotes that friends and family retell with affection rather than criticism.

More importantly, this quirk has shaped how I approach communication in all areas of my life. The strategies I've developed—creating distraction-free environments, maintaining eye contact, repeating information, asking clarifying questions, quieting my internal dialogue—have become strengths rather than just compensatory techniques. They have made me a more attentive listener, a more precise communicator, and a more empathetic conversational partner.

I still occasionally mishear or misinterpret what others say. But these incidents now elicit laughter rather than embarrassment, both from me and from those who know me well enough to expect these occasional linguistic detours. In embracing this aspect of myself, I've come to see it not as a deficiency to be hidden but as a unique characteristic that contributes to who I am. It has taught me patience with myself and others, highlighted the importance of clear communication, and provided countless moments of unexpected humor in everyday interactions.

And sometimes, when saying goodbye to my father on the phone, I still sign off with "Avagadang to you, mate!" It's our private joke, a reminder of how a simple misunderstanding can become a cherished memory, a symbol of the unique ways we each experience and interpret the world around us.

So maybe there are still some Fraggles in my ears after all—not dust bunnies who scramble messages, but little reminders that communication is complex, that hearing isn't the same as understanding, and that sometimes the most meaningful connections come from our most human moments of misunderstanding.

Because here's the truth, friend: We ALL mishear, misinterpret, and misunderstand sometimes. My version might be more dramatic or frequent, but none of us gets it right all the time. And in acknowledging that, in developing tools to bridge those gaps, we create space for deeper connection and more authentic communication.

So the next time you find yourself in a conversation where something seems off, where the response doesn't quite match the question, take a breath and consider that maybe—just maybe—there are some Fraggles at work. And then, with patience and humor, find your way back to understanding.

Avagadang to you, mate! (That means "wishing you crystal-clear communication" in my personal dictionary.)

The Courage to Prioritize Your Own Well-being

"Mommy, I want waffle."

That's how my mornings begin most days—not with gentle birdsong or the peaceful ritual of stretching in quiet solitude like those Instagram influencers with their perfect morning routines. NOPE. It's tiny humans hovering inches from my face, demanding breakfast before my eyelids have fully separated.

Can I get an amen from the mama crowd?

Here's a truth bomb I've had to face: I often put EVERYONE else at the top of my list. As a mom, I think it just comes naturally. If the kids need something, I take care of it before I get to anything else. And it's not just the kids. My husband will ask me to email someone or remind me of something and then off I go. It's basically everything and everyone else first, and then me—if there's anything left, which there rarely is.

The pattern begins before I even step out of bed. Most mornings, I open my eyes to a small face inches from mine, already making demands. Sometimes it's breakfast, sometimes it's help finding a phone that they DESPERATELY need at 5:47 AM, sometimes it's just wanting attention. My own morning routine—that quiet cup of coffee, those few minutes to collect my thoughts, that brief moment of stillness before the day begins—becomes an afterthought, something to squeeze in between attending to everyone else's needs.

You know that fantasy where you wake up before everyone else and enjoy a peaceful moment to yourself? I've tried it. And it works on most days. However, sometimes, in my house, the children seem to have some sort of sixth sense that alerts them the moment my consciousness returns. It's like they have a "Mom's Awake" alarm that goes off in their little brains.

"The human has opened her eyes! ATTACK WITH DEMANDS!"

This tendency used to extend beyond my home life, too. When I worked a corporate remote job, I would respond to emails before completing my priority tasks. Someone else's need always seemed more urgent and worthy of immediate attention than my own requirements for basic self-care and professional effectiveness.

What makes this pattern so sneaky is how NATURAL it felt. The narrative of the selfless mother, the accommodating colleague, the ever-available friend is so deeply ingrained that deviating from it used to trigger immediate guilt. When I did occasionally put my needs first, I'd find myself offering elaborate explanations, as if requiring basic self-maintenance needs justification.

"Sorry I can't volunteer for your event this week—I have this crazy thing that came up. But I feel TERRIBLE about it!"

Then I got to thinking about that airplane analogy—you know the one. When you're in an emergency, they tell you to put on your oxygen mask first before you help someone else. I've also heard it said that you can't pour from an empty cup. And both of those analogies are seriously PLAYED OUT. But their essence is still so true.

The problem is, no one tells you how hard it is to put that oxygen mask on.

Why Is This So Hard? (No, Really—Why?)

But it's SO HARD, especially when you have children, to put yourself at the top of your list; it seems selfish. It seems self-centered. It seems like you're insensitive or inconsiderate. It just doesn't seem the natural way to do things when you have to care for other people. To serve other people, you must put them ahead of you, right? At least, that's what the world has made us believe.

The conflict is both internal and external. Internally, years of conditioning have linked self-prioritization with selfishness in my mind. There's that voice that whispers, "How can you take time for yourself when your child needs help with homework?" or "How can you decline that request when your friend is clearly overwhelmed?" This internal critic is RELENTLESS, questioning every attempt at self-care as potential evidence of moral failure.

It's like having a tiny judgmental roommate living in your head, one who's memorized every guilt-inducing message society has ever created and loves to recite them at maximum volume whenever you consider doing something just for yourself.

"Oh, you want to take a bath? BY YOURSELF? Pee ALONE? What kind of monster ARE you?"

Externally, the responses to boundary-setting can reinforce these doubts. The raised eyebrow when you mention needing personal time. The subtle guilt trips. The "I thought I could count on you" comments.

The paradox, of course, is that this approach ultimately

serves NO ONE. Not our children, who benefit from seeing healthy boundaries. Not our partners, who deserve a relationship with someone who isn't perpetually depleted. Not our friends, who need us at our best. And certainly not ourselves, as we gradually erode our capacity for joy, creativity, and true presence.

If I am depleted, suffering, tired, and exhausted, I definitely can't give something that I do not have. If I'm not full of energy, I can't give it to someone else. If I'm so weak, I can't help strengthen someone else. If I can't move, I can't help carry someone else. If I am not nourished, I can't give nourishment to someone else.

For example, if I didn't take my vitamins, or eat properly, when I nursed my son, he wouldn't get the proper nutrients that he needed from me. He got whatever my body could scrape together, which could have been approximately three molecules of calcium and whatever was left of yesterday's Starbuck's.

The same is true as it relates to everything in my life. I won't give my best to a project if I'm not in the best state of mind. And how can I achieve that if I do not put myself first? If I'm not well rested, I may not be coordinated enough to carry out assignments, speak in engagements, and even be of help to anyone around me.

I've experienced this reality firsthand. There was a period when I was running on minimal sleep, skipping meals to accommodate everyone else's schedules, and saying yes to every request. The result wasn't superhuman productivity or exceptional caregiving. It was missed details, forgotten appointments, short temper, and a pervasive fog that made even simple tasks feel overwhelming.

I wasn't giving more of myself; I was giving a depleted, diminished version of myself. I was the human equivalent of those last few watery squirts from an almost-empty ketchup bottle. Nobody wants that on their emotional hamburger.

However, it's easier to say "put yourself first" than to actually do it. So many things come into play when you are actually required to put yourself first. Your mind may play tricks on you and make you believe that you're being a little too selfish. You may even feel like that other thing is much more important than you at that time. Sometimes, you may be so weak and stressed out, but you tell yourself: "I think I can stretch a little further." And that's a total lie.

Breaking Free From the Guilt Prison

If we get rid of the shame, fear, and worry that goes along with wanting to put ourselves first, I think it will be an easier concept to grasp. I think women oftentimes feel as though we must put everybody else's needs and wants ahead of our own. I've been guilty of doing that in my life. So, I'm deliberately working on putting myself first.

Breaking this cycle of guilt requires CONSCIOUS EFFORT to recognize and challenge these guilt triggers. It means actively reframing self-care not as indulgence but as responsible stewardship of the resources—physical, emotional, mental—that enable us to show up fully in all areas of our lives.

Some say you should put God first. To me, that goes without saying. To me, God is a constant. God is the center. Everything flows from God. God is the source of all life; everything that exists is by Him and His power. God is not to be taken away and replaced with something or someone else, not even me. In my life, God is a foundation, so I don't have to put Him first because He's always there in my life. He's just like air—you do not decide when you need air or don't. He is simply a constant reality. My priorities can shift all the time because I can be doing different things, but God is not a shift in priority. God is who He is, and He's always going to be that in my life that never leaves or moves.

This spiritual framing has been crucial in my journey toward healthier self-prioritization. Understanding God not as a competing priority but as the underlying foundation of all priorities removes the false dichotomy between serving God and caring for the self. In this framework, proper self-care becomes an act of stewardship, a recognition that my body, mind, and spirit are gifts to be nurtured rather than resources to be exploited until depletion.

When Everyone Gets the Leftover Scraps of You

If I don't give myself what I need, then everyone else is going to get pieces of me. Not the whole of who I am. No one will be able to get the best of me. This means if I haven't taken time to rest, reflect, rejuvenate, re-strategize, meditate, eat, sleep, or just BREATHE, somebody might get a cranky me, somebody might get a bitchy me, somebody might get a hungry me, somebody might get a tired me. Somebody might get a stressed-out me.

Let's be real – nobody wants the version of me that hasn't eaten in six hours and had to repeat the same instruction seventeen times. That version of me makes toddler tantrums look reasonable and measured.

I've seen this play out in my own life in ways both subtle and dramatic. There was the time I snapped at my child for a minor infraction because I had been running on four hours of sleep for days. The time I made a significant error on a project because I hadn't taken a break in hours and my brain was foggy. The time I burst into tears during a minor disagreement with my husband because I had been ignoring my own emotional needs for weeks.

Each of these moments represented not just a failure of self-regulation but a failure of self-care. I wasn't giving pieces of myself in those moments; I was giving the WORST of myself, the version least equipped to respond with wisdom, patience, or clarity.

But if I am full, rejuvenated, satisfied, and have taken time to fill my cup, then I can run over and pour into someone else. They won't be getting remnants of who I am.

The contrast is stark and unmistakable. When I've slept well, eaten properly, moved my body, and had moments of solitude and reflection, I bring a different quality of presence to every interaction. I listen more attentively. I respond more thoughtfully. I create more effectively. I love more abundantly. The version of me that emerges from proper self-care isn't just getting by—she's THRIVING, and that vitality ripples outward to benefit everyone she encounters.

Taking Back Your Time (Yes, It's Actually Yours)

So, I think it's very important to change and shift the mindset of putting yourself at the top of your list. Prioritizing yourself is a priority. And sometimes that means taking your time.

The whole notion of taking your time is to lay hold of your time, deliberately. It means that you have to steal away; you have to grab your time, you have to insist upon your alone time.

To get alone with yourself
to center yourself
to ground yourself
to engage in self-care
to engage in self-love
to engage in self-growth
to engage in self-awareness.

The language here is intentionally active: steal, grab, insist. These verbs recognize the reality that time for self-care isn't typically offered freely in our busy, demanding world. It must be claimed, sometimes against resistance, both internal and external. It requires assertion, boundaries, and, occasionally, an unapologetic stance.

Because if I don't do those things, someone else will take it, something else will take it. Even sitting and being idle is a form of self-care. Because taking my time doesn't necessarily say what I should fill it with. It just says, "I'm going to take my time." And why is that? "It is because it is mine to take when I need to and when I actually want to."

So I can decide to say: "I'm going to take my time and exercise." Or "I'm going to take my time and drink a glass of water." Or "I'm going to take my time and read a book." "I'm going to take my time and meditate." Or "I'm going to take my time and go to the coffee shop." Or "I'm going to take my time and go shopping." Or "I'm just going to take my time and do whatever I want to do." Or "I'm just going to take my time and do NOTHING! And whatever I'm going to do with that time is my own business."

This reclamation of time is revolutionary in a culture that prizes constant productivity and availability. The radical act isn't necessarily in how we use the time but in asserting our right to claim it at all. Whether the time is used for meditation or Netflix, journaling or napping, the essential element is the recognition that our time belongs first to us, not to the demands and expectations of others.

When Peace Becomes Your Protector

I've had a profound revelation lately that has turned my whole understanding upside down: peace doesn't actually need my protection. If I prioritize it, peace will protect ME.

It's the most beautiful reciprocal relationship I never fully understood until now. The Bible makes reference to this—peace standing guard over our hearts and minds. All this time, I've been thinking I needed to defend my peace like it was some fragile thing that could be shattered at any moment. But that's backward thinking. Peace isn't the vulnerable one in this relationship—I am.

This shift in perspective feels like putting down a heavy shield I've been carrying for years. I was exhausting myself trying to protect something that, when properly cultivated, was designed to protect me.

I've noticed over the past year that stress has made me physically sick—sleepless nights, anxiety attacks, constant worry. The stress was everywhere—in the media, in my environment, and so much of it self-induced. I was trying so hard to guard my peace that I was actually creating more chaos in the process. It's like frantically running around the house checking the locks over and over when what you really need is to sit down and rest in the safety you already have.

Prioritizing peace isn't just emotional self-care—it's preventative healthcare. It's recognizing that the body keeps score, that every "yes" that depletes us, every boundary violation we permit, every need we ignore has a cumulative effect on our physical well-being. But rather than seeing this as a battle where I have to fight off every stress-inducing element, I now see it as an invitation to create space for peace to do its work.

Someone very close to me is a worrier. She will overwhelm you with her worries. That's why I can't talk to her for too long. I used to think I was protecting my peace by avoiding her calls, but now I understand that when I prioritize peace in my life, it gives me the wisdom to know my limits. Peace isn't something I'm desperately clutching—it's the gentle hand guiding my decisions.

That doesn't mean I won't listen to a good vent or be a shoulder to cry on. It just means that I understand the difference between compassion and absorption. I can be present for others without taking on their emotional state as my own.

This boundary around emotional energy is perhaps one of the most challenging to establish, particularly for women who have been socialized to be emotional caretakers. The expectation that we should always be available to absorb others' feelings, to provide comfort and support regardless of our own emotional state, runs deep.

Yet emotional energy is a finite resource. Being present for others in their distress requires capacity that isn't always available if we're depleted ourselves. Recognizing this limitation isn't callous; it's realistic. It acknowledges that true support requires resources, and those resources need replenishment.

When I prioritize peace, it stands as a guardian at the door of my mind and heart, helping me discern what to let in and what to leave outside. It's not that I'm turning away from the world or its troubles—I'm simply allowing peace to help me engage with it in a way that doesn't destroy me in the process.

I'm not even forty yet. I haven't seen Hawaii or learned how to swim. There are so many things I want to do. I try not to let the news consume my thoughts but at the same time I want to stay aware. Peace doesn't ask me to hide from reality—it equips me to face it with clarity and strength.

My Daily Priority Check-In System

Right now in my life, I have kids, I have a marriage, I'm in school (almost done, thank you Jesus!), I operate a nonprofit, and I'm a business owner. Those priorities need evaluating daily. They all need my attention. Sometimes they even need my undivided attention. But what I am learning to do is this: every single day, I check in with myself (FIRST) by setting my alarm before everyone wakes up and I go to my office and pray, I check in with my spouse, I check in with my children. I look at my priorities as far as work is concerned and I look at my priorities as far as school. Sometimes those can be interchangeable between work or school then school or work. I don't put my children ahead of my husband, and I try not to put everybody else on top of me.

This daily priority check-in has become a crucial practice. It's not rigid or formulaic; it's a flexible assessment that acknowledges the changing demands of each day. Some days, my graduate studies truly do need to take precedence over business matters. Some days, my child's needs are genuinely more urgent than my husband's. The key is that these decisions are made consciously, not by default, and always with an awareness of the sustainability of the pattern.

That's growth.

That's coming to terms with how it should be done and

actually doing it.

The distinction between knowing and doing is significant. Many of us intellectually understand the importance of self-care and healthy boundaries but struggle to implement these principles consistently in our daily lives. The gap between understanding and action is where real transformation occurs, where abstract principles become lived reality.

You know why this is important? Because, at times, climbing out from under other unsorted priorities is VERY HARD. It feels like I'm suffocating. Like I can't breathe. It even feels like it is impossible to do.

That is a signal that I have not properly prioritized my life.

My room is a mess. My house is cluttered. I know when my priorities are out of whack because everything else becomes out of whack. So, for me, God is at the center, then me, next my husband, then children, the family and everything else can follow.

The physical manifestations of misaligned priorities—the cluttered home, the neglected spaces—are often the most visible indicators that something is amiss in our internal order. These external signs serve as valuable feedback, alerting us to the need for recalibration before more serious consequences emerge.

When I Learned the Hard Way (And You Don't Have To)

I will never forget the time when I was working for a friend of mine. At first, working with her was a great idea. It felt right. It felt productive. I felt like I was accomplishing something. However, pretty soon, I would get emails, phone calls, and texts at ALL times of the day and night. Everything that was on fire for my friend was suddenly on fire for me too. My friend and her work became more of a priority than it should have been. That put a strain on everything else that I had to do in my life.

It was like adopting her emergency as a 24/7 foster emergency. "Oh, you have a crisis? Let me drop EVERYTHING to make it my crisis too!"

It put a strain on my marriage and it put a strain on my relationship and activities with my children. It put a strain on my creativity; it put a strain on EVERYTHING that concerned me. I had to shut several different things off in my life in order to work on the things that were hot and burning for her. I would exhaust all of my efforts and energy on projects that had to do with this person.

The insidious nature of priority creep cannot be overstated. It rarely happens all at once. Instead, it's a gradual erosion of boundaries, a slow reordering of priorities that occurs so incrementally we barely notice until we're in too deep. What begins as occasional after-hours emails becomes an expectation of 24/7 availability. What starts as a temporary intensification of work demands becomes the new normal.

In this particular situation, there was also the complicating factor of friendship. Professional boundaries are already challenging to maintain; when personal relationships overlap with professional ones, those boundaries become even more complex to navigate. The fear of damaging the friendship made it harder to assert limits around work expectations.

When it was time for me to focus on myself or focus on things that I wanted to do, I simply couldn't do it. And it was because I had exhausted all of my efforts and drive working on someone else's vision.

This depletion of creative and emotional energy represents

a particularly painful consequence of boundary failure. When we pour our limited resources into others' priorities, we often find ourselves with nothing left for our own dreams and aspirations. The projects that matter most to us, the creative endeavors that bring us joy, the personal goals that align with our values—these are frequently the first casualties of overcommitment to others' needs.

The Value of "Not My Emergency"

It wasn't until I realized my worth and my value that I insisted upon prioritizing myself. It wasn't her fault; it was MY fault for not setting proper boundaries. I've learned that if something is on fire for someone, that does not mean that it has to be on fire for me. If something is an emergency for someone else it doesn't mean that that's my emergency. That does not make me selfish or insensitive. If anything, that's the most realistic thing to do most times.

This realization—that others' emergencies aren't automatically our emergencies—is transformative. It doesn't diminish the genuine nature of their urgency; it simply acknowledges that not every crisis requires our immediate response, especially when that response comes at the expense of our well-being or other priorities.

When my kids have been sick, when I've had to rush somebody to the emergency room, everybody else in the world did not stop what they were doing to make my emergency their emergency as well. No, it was my emergency alone. It had to be.

This perspective shift has been crucial—recognizing that just as others don't drop everything for my emergencies, I'm not obligated to drop everything for theirs. This isn't selfishness; it's reality. It's an acknowledgment that each of us has our own sphere of primary responsibility, and while we support each other, we can't and shouldn't take on everyone else's priorities as our own.

So, with clients or with friends or with family, setting those proper boundaries now sounds a little like: "Hey I've got a few other things that I'm doing first and if I have time and if I have the capacity to be able to address that today, I will address it today. But if I don't, I'm not going to be able to get to that today. So, maybe I'll get to that tomorrow."

Having to be able to say that took a little bit of work because I had a really huge problem with disappointing people. It's the people-pleaser in me that I work on daily. I don't want to disappoint anyone in my life. I don't want to make anyone feel bad, especially somebody that I consider a friend.

The fear of disappointing others, particularly those we care about, is one of the most powerful forces preventing healthy boundary-setting. It's rooted in both empathy (we genuinely don't want others to feel let down) and fear (we worry about the relational consequences of saying no). Overcoming this fear requires recognizing that disappointment is a normal, survivable emotion that others can and will move through. It also requires trusting that relationships built on mutual respect can withstand the occasional boundary assertion.

However, it wouldn't have been doing her any good or service if I were doing something with a chip on my shoulder because I couldn't set those proper boundaries. I can't tell you how many times I've been upset with people who had no idea they were encroaching on my life's priorities. That is so silly but it happens all the time. It takes practice to express boundaries, to allow others to understand your feelings, and to be okay with their response.

When It's Actually My Fault (And That's Okay)

I had to tell the story and retell the story and retell this story to myself because initially, when I began to tell it, I felt that I had no fault in it. It was my friend's fault. She should have been able to know that I was being stretched too thin. She shouldn't have expected me to work that hard for her. How could she not be considerate of me?

The truth is if I didn't want to accept the work, I should have said no in the first place.

This shift from blaming others to accepting responsibility for our own boundaries is transformative. While it's true that some people may take advantage of our willingness to help, or may not be sensitive to signs of overload, ultimately we are the ones who must communicate our limits clearly. Others cannot be expected to read our minds or intuit our capacity.

Taking responsibility doesn't mean blaming ourselves for boundary violations or feeling guilty about needing limits. It simply means acknowledging our agency in the situation—recognizing that, in most cases, we have more power to change the dynamic than we initially believe.

Setting proper boundaries with people means that I've got to open my mouth. I have to say "no" sometimes. I have to sometimes say "it's not really convenient for me to do that." I have to rise beyond sentiments that bring guilt. I have to walk away sometimes. I have to say "not right now" and that means being able to be self-aware and know that "hey I don't have capacity for this thing right now…."

My Monday Sanctuary

I decided to take Mondays off. Being in corporate for so long, I dreaded Mondays. Monday! Whenever it came, I hated it. I think it's because Sunday would take so much energy from me. I would serve in church and Sundays were more like a busy day. It felt like I never really had a day to regroup on the weekend. By Friday you're coming off a work day and Saturday is the day you kind of get to relax but, not really. Then here comes Monday when you have to start your work week.

Again.

The creation of this Monday sanctuary represents a concrete application of the principle of self-prioritization. It's not just philosophical or theoretical—it's a specific, practical decision to carve out space solely for replenishment. It acknowledges the reality that serving others, whether in church or in family life, requires energy that must be restored.

Now that I work for myself and I have autonomy over my schedule, I say Mondays are for ME. I don't take any meetings. I don't focus on any business. I take my Mondays for me and me alone. If I choose to take a meeting, it's because I prioritize it for that day. I typically clear my schedule on Mondays. I don't do anything or I do something that brings my soul joy. I block my calendar. That is my day to refocus and regroup and re-strategize. And unless something is literally on fire, then I'm not running for that. That is something that I set as a non-negotiable for me, several years ago. And I'm glad I did!

The concept of "non-negotiable" self-care is powerful. It elevates certain practices from "nice if I can fit it in" to "essential component of my well-being." Just as we wouldn't consider skipping meals or sleep as optional, designating certain forms of self-care as non-negotiable acknowledges

From Passive Recipient to Active Designer of Your Life

I'm finding it more useful to hold myself accountable to the things that I say that I'm going to do. That means prioritizing me in my schedule, prioritizing myself in my life. That means being an active participant and not just allowing life to happen to me. Being an active participant in my life involves my being mindful and intentional about my priorities daily.

The shift from passive recipient of life's demands to active architect of one's schedule and priorities represents a profound reclamation of agency. It rejects the narrative that self-sacrifice is inevitable, particularly for women and caregivers, and asserts instead that we have both the right and the responsibility to shape our lives according to our values and needs.

Even though my priorities shift at times, the constants—the mainstays in my life are God, my marriage and my family. Those things will never change. One thing I keep at the forefront of my mind is how what I am doing matters. I tell myself these things:

I am important!

I matter!

I give myself permission to put myself first.

These affirmations aren't just positive thinking—they're declarations of value that counter the pervasive messaging that our needs are secondary. They represent a conscious rejection of the martyr mentality that has been particularly encouraged in women, and an embrace instead of the truth that our well-being is not just important but essential to fulfilling our purpose and serving those we love.

In the end, putting myself first isn't about selfishness. It's about stewardship—recognizing that my energy, creativity, health, and joy are resources to be carefully tended rather than endlessly exploited. It's about sustainability—acknowledging that a pattern of perpetual self-neglect eventually yields diminishing returns for everyone involved. And it's about authenticity—honoring the truth that I can only give from a place of fullness when I've attended to my own needs with the same care and attention I offer others.

The airplane oxygen mask analogy might be overused, but its wisdom remains: securing our own well-being first isn't selfish—it's the only way to ensure we have anything worthwhile to offer those we care about most.

And sometimes, it means letting the waffles wait while you have your coffee first.

Permission Slip for Your Soul

I want to talk to you directly for a moment, friend to friend. If no one has told you this lately—or ever—let me be the one to say it: You have permission to put yourself on your own priority list. Not at the bottom. Not as an afterthought. Right at the top, alongside the people and values that matter most to you.

You have permission to say no without a ten-paragraph explanation.

You have permission to take a day off without spending it catching up on household chores.

You have permission to put your phone on Do Not Disturb and ignore the little red notification bubbles that are designed specifically to hijack your attention.

You have permission to serve store-bought cookies at the

school bake sale.

You have permission to cancel plans when you're exhausted.

You have permission to prioritize sleep over inbox zero.

You have permission to leave some things undone.

This isn't about abdicating responsibility or neglecting the people who depend on you. It's about recognizing that you can't fulfill those responsibilities or show up for those people if you're running on fumes. It's about acknowledging that your needs aren't optional extras to be addressed "someday" when everyone else's needs have been met. They're essential requirements for your functioning and flourishing.

I know it's not easy. I know the guilt monsters are loud. I know the to-do list is long. I know the expectations (both external and internal) can feel crushing. But I also know this: small, consistent acts of self-prioritization create powerful ripple effects.

When you honor your needs, you model for your children what healthy self-regard looks like. When you set boundaries, you teach others how to treat you. When you take time to replenish, you bring a fuller, more present version of yourself to every interaction.

Start small if you need to. Five minutes of solitude with your coffee before the morning chaos begins. A genuine "no" to one request that would deplete you. A brief walk alone to clear your head. These small acts of self-care may feel insignificant, but they're revolutionary in a culture that tells women, especially mothers, that their needs should always come last.

Consider this your permission slip, signed and sealed. Keep it close. Pull it out when the guilt creeps in. Remember that taking care of yourself isn't selfish—it's the foundation for everything else you want to give and do and be in this world.

And on those days when the permission slip feels flimsy against the weight of expectations? Reach out. Connect with other women who are walking this same path. Share your struggles. Celebrate your boundaries. Remind each other that this journey of self-prioritization isn't something we have to figure out alone.

Because here's the truth: When we collectively decide that our well-being matters, when we refuse to accept depletion as the price of worthiness, we don't just change our own lives. We change the narrative for every woman who comes after us. We create a new story about what it means to love others well while honoring ourselves fully.

And that's not just good for us—it's good for everyone whose lives we touch.

So go ahead. Have that uninterrupted cup of coffee. Take that bath. Set that boundary. Claim that Monday. Your well-being is worth it. YOU are worth it.

And the waffles can wait.

When Pain Becomes Purpose

Okay, so here's the thing about purpose—it has ZERO respect for your carefully crafted five-year plan. Trust me on this one.

The year was 2018, and I was deep in the trenches of what I lovingly call "controlled chaos parenting." Four of our then-ten kids were at different schools, developmental stages, and drama levels. I had my color-coded calendar in my head, my meal-prepping system that ended up being whatever I could manage to put together quickly, and my "mommy needs Twizzlers" emergency stash hidden where even my boys (human vacuum cleaners) couldn't find it.

I wasn't on some spiritual quest to find my life's purpose. I wasn't meditating on mountaintops or journaling my prayer list to God. I was just trying to make sure everyone had clean underwear and maybe, just maybe, remember to shave my legs occasionally.

That's the funny thing about purpose—sometimes it's not wearing a neon sign saying "YOUR DESTINY IS HERE!" Sometimes it walks right through your front door, looking suspiciously like your everyday life falling completely apart.

My daughter Genesis had just started middle school that year, which is already emotional whiplash under normal circumstances. But our "normal" had been redefined over the previous two years as she fought an autoimmune disease that attacked her brain. Let that sink in. My vibrant, dance-any-and-everywhere girl had spent years in hospitals, pumped full of medications that saved her life but changed her appearance dramatically.

Those steroids? Miracle workers and appearance wreckers. They caused significant swelling throughout her body, completely transforming how she looked. In elementary school, this hadn't mattered much. Everyone knew Genesis. They knew her story. They protected her.

Middle school, though? That's the Hunger Games with homework.

A Mother's Heartbreak

Each morning before school, I'd help Genesis get ready, filling her emotional tank with affirmations that would make any self-help guru proud:

"You are beautiful." "You are strong." "You are worthy of respect." "Anyone who can't see your beauty needs their eyes checked."

I believed—perhaps naively—that her inner light was so bright, her spirit so genuinely kind, that others would naturally be drawn to her regardless of her appearance. I had conveniently forgotten the wasteland of social awareness that is middle school.

I remember exactly where I was standing when my purpose found me. At the bottom of our hill, watching Genesis trudge home, shoulders hunched, face streaked with tears. The image burned itself into my memory—this child who had faced death with courage, who had kept smiling through treatments that would break most adults, had been shattered by the casual cruelty of kids who had no idea what she'd been through.

"They called me fat," she whispered. "They said I look like a balloon."

In that moment, I experienced a tornado of emotions—blinding mama-bear rage, gut-wrenching heartbreak, and a strange moment of recognition. I saw myself in her tears. I remembered being that girl, the one whose confidence was dismantled brick by brick by careless comments and deliberate exclusion. The girl who took decades to rebuild what should never have been damaged in the first place.

I'm not a violent person, but I'll admit that for a brief moment, I contemplated behaviors that would definitely have made the local news. "MOM OF TEN STORMS MIDDLE SCHOOL, THREATENS PRETEENS WITH EMOTIONAL INTELLIGENCE TRAINING."

Instead, I did what any reasonable, slightly unhinged mother would do—I hugged my girl, made her favorite snack, and then stayed up until 2 AM crafting what was essentially a rage-post on Facebook.

The Birth of a Vision

Here's something you should know about me: I'm a fixer. When the toaster breaks, I'm watching YouTube tutorials before the bread has even cooled. When there's a problem with no solution, my brain goes into overdrive until I create one. It's equal parts superpower and exhausting personality trait.

I'd already gone through the "proper channels" at school. I'd had the meetings, filed the reports, listened to administrators promise to "monitor the situation." Meanwhile, my daughter was inventing stomach aches to avoid school and no longer looked in mirrors.

So there I was, rage-typing at 2 AM:

"What if there was an event where girls could come together to celebrate who they are? Where they could see examples of strong women from all walks of life? Where confidence wasn't treated like some magical unicorn quality but a muscle that can be developed? I'm talking workshops, speakers, poetry, music, dance, art—a full day of 'You are amazing exactly as you are' energy! Is anyone else thinking this needs to exist?"

I posted it thinking maybe a few friends would sympathize or offer to bring cookies to this hypothetical event. I was not prepared for what happened next.

My phone nearly exploded with notifications. Comments. Private messages. Shares. Women I barely knew were sending their stories, offering venues, volunteering as speakers. Local businesses wanted to donate supplies. I had accidentally tapped into something much bigger than my daughter's experience—I had uncovered a collective wound that was desperate for healing.

From Idea to Reality

I'll be painfully honest here: I had no clue what I was doing. Zero. Zilch. Nada.

I'd never planned a major event, never started an organization, never even led a committee at the PTA because, let's be real, those women are intimidating and I once brought store-bought cookies to the bake sale. (The horror!)

Every day brought new challenges that made me question my sanity. Budgets. Insurance. Marketing. Registration systems. There were moments I found myself hiding in my pantry, stress-eating the emergency chocolate and wondering if I'd bitten off way more than I could chew.

What saved me was a coffee meeting with a woman who later became a mentor. I was spiraling, listing all the ways this could fail, when she calmly reached across the table, took my color-coded to-do list, and said:

"Don't worry about the how. Focus on the what."

Those words hit me like a lightning bolt. The "what" was clear: creating a space where girls like Genesis could rebuild their confidence, connect with others, and see examples of resilient women who had overcome their own challenges. When I focused on that, the "how" seemed to fall into place—often in ways I never could have planned.

The first You Go Girl summit happened four months later. Over 200 girls and women gathered for a day that still gives me goosebumps when I think about it. The energy in that room was electric—a beautiful storm of vulnerability, inspiration, and collective empowerment.

And Genesis? My girl who had been hiding from mirrors? By the end of the day, she was standing taller. Smiling—a real smile that reached her eyes. Connecting with other girls who were fighting their own battles. Something shifted in her that day, and in me too.

The Ripple Effect

What started as a Facebook rant from a fed-up mom transformed into a full-blown nonprofit organization that, years later, continues to grow in ways I never imagined.

The annual summit expanded to include after-school workshops, mentoring relationships, and career programs for women. We developed programming for different age groups, from elementary girls just beginning to encounter social pressures to high school students preparing for adult independence.

The impact stories are what keep me going on the hard days (and trust me, there are still plenty of hard days). The shy girl who found her voice. The teen who confessed she had been a bully herself and transformed into an anti-bullying ambassador at her school. The mother-daughter pairs who rebuilt fractured relationships through shared experiences.

And Genesis? That swollen, tear-stained face I saw coming up the hill is now the face of a confident young woman who uses her story to help others. The medical challenges that once made her a target have become part of her testimony of resilience.

Purpose Through Pain

Before this chapter of my life, I was like a lot of people—vaguely dissatisfied, feeling like I was meant for "something more" but not quite sure what that looked like. I was scanning job boards, taking personality tests, reading books with titles like "Find Your Passion in 30 Days or Less!" (Spoiler alert: Those don't work.)

The truth that nobody wants to hear is that sometimes the pathway to purpose runs straight through pain. Not the cute, Instagram-worthy kind of challenge that makes for a good motivational caption. The gut-wrenching, bring-you-to-your-knees kind that breaks you open and forces you to rebuild.

Would I choose this path again if given the option? That's complicated. No parent would willingly subject their child to suffering. I would give anything to have spared Genesis the medical challenges and social cruelty she endured.

But I've come to recognize that the very experiences I would have avoided at all costs became the soil in which my purpose took root. The advocacy skills I developed fighting for Genesis's medical care. The fierce protectiveness that drove me to action. The empathy developed through our shared pain. All of these became essential tools for the work I now do.

Overcoming Limiting Beliefs

Once the initial excitement of starting You Go Girl faded, the doubters emerged:

"There are already so many girl-empowerment programs. Is another one really necessary?"

"You should see about working at Girls Inc."

"Do you have any actual qualifications to be doing this work?"

"This is a lot to take on with all the kids you have. Maybe you should wait until they're older."

Some of these comments came from well-meaning friends concerned about my workload. Others came from established community leaders who weren't thrilled about a newcomer in their territory. Some were just practical questions that needed addressing.

The voices of doubt weren't just external—the loudest critic often lived in my own head, usually speaking at 3 AM when I couldn't sleep:

"Who do you think you are?" "What if you fail publicly?" "What if you make things worse instead of better?"

I had to learn to distinguish between constructive feedback that could improve our programs and limiting beliefs that would derail them entirely. When someone suggested we needed more diverse representation among our speakers, that was valuable input. When someone said girls don't really need special programming anymore because "haven't we solved gender inequality?", that was a limiting belief contradicted by both research and lived experience.

Purpose as Divine Calling

At the risk of getting a little spiritual on you, I've come to see purpose not just as something we create but as something we uncover—a divine assignment uniquely suited to our specific gifts, experiences, and passions.

This perspective changes everything. When I view You Go Girl not as "my project" but as work I've been called to do, it shifts the weight of responsibility. I don't have to be perfect; I just have to be faithful to the calling. I don't have to have all the answers; I just need to remain open to guidance.

Even Genesis's illness—as devastating as it was—becomes part of a larger narrative when viewed through this lens. The empathy, advocacy skills, and perspective developed through that season equipped me precisely for the work I now do with girls and women. Nothing is wasted.

This spiritual framework provides both motivation and sustainability. On the days when I'm exhausted, when funding is tight, when problems seem insurmountable, I return to the conviction that this is work I've been entrusted to do. There's something bigger than me at work here.

The work of empowering girls and women isn't just about personal confidence or individual success—though these are important—but about creating communities and eventually a world that more fully reflects what's possible when everyone is able to develop and share their gifts without the constraints of diminished self-worth or limiting expectations.

Purpose found me through pain, clarified itself through action, and continues to evolve through community. My role is to remain open, responsive, and faithful to the calling, trusting that the same force that initiated this journey will sustain it through whatever challenges and opportunities lie ahead.

So if you're still searching for your purpose, maybe stop looking so hard. Look around instead. The very challenge that's breaking your heart might be the doorway to the work you were born to do.

Walking Through the Fire

Here's what I've learned about purpose that most inspirational Instagram quotes won't tell you: it's HARD. Like, ugly-cry-in-your-car-between-meetings hard. Like questioning-everything-at-2AM hard. Like wondering-if-you've-made-a-terrible-mistake hard.

The day after our first summit, I crashed. Hard. The adrenaline that had carried me through months of planning evaporated, leaving me exhausted, emotional, and suddenly terrified by the realization that people were counting on this to continue. What if it had been a fluke? What if I couldn't recreate the magic? What if I'd accidentally started something I couldn't sustain?

In those moments of doubt (and there were many), I learned to return to the source of it all—that moment at the bottom of the hill with Genesis. The tears on her face. The determination that rose up within me. The conviction that no child should have their spirit broken by cruelty they didn't deserve.

When we connect to the original pain that birthed our purpose, we find the strength to keep going even when the path gets impossibly steep.

I've watched Genesis transform from a girl who hid from mirrors to a young woman who steps confidently in front of audiences to share her story. I've seen her use the very experiences that once broke her heart to help heal others. And in her transformation, I've found confirmation that this work—despite all its challenges—is exactly what I'm meant to be doing.

Your purpose might be waiting in the most painful chapter of your story. The question isn't whether you'll encounter that pain—we all do—but what you'll build with it. Will you let it define you, or will you use it to define a new possibility for yourself and others?

The choice is yours. And while I can't promise the journey will be easy, I can promise it will be worth it.

Motherhood Unfiltered

I had my first kid at age 21. That's not when I became a mother.

Let that sink in for a second. I was barely legal to order a margarita, still figuring out who the heck I was supposed to be as an adult, and suddenly there was this tiny human who needed me for *literally everything*. Talk about a record-scratch moment in life's soundtrack.

Here's the truth bomb I've come to understand: there's a profound difference between being a mom and becoming a mother. Being a mom? That happens in an instant—the moment that pregnancy test shows two lines, or when you sign adoption papers, or when you commit to raising a child who needs you. Boom. Mom status: achieved.

But motherhood? That's a whole different journey. One that unfolds over time, through sleepless nights and first steps, through tears (theirs and yours) and triumphs, through moments when you have absolutely no idea what you're doing but somehow make it through anyway.

I remember that first night home from the hospital like it was yesterday. The nurses and doctors who had been my safety net were gone. It was just me and this new life, staring at each other in the quiet darkness. The love was there, absolutely, but swimming alongside it was a current of pure terror and a flood of "what have I gotten myself into?" thoughts that I wasn't prepared for.

I'd held babies before. Changed diapers for cousins. Even babysat for days at a time. But this? This was *forever*. This was all-encompassing in a way my 21-year-old brain couldn't fully comprehend.

Let me be clear about something: if you've carried a life in your womb, you're a mom. Period. Whether that baby came into this world or not, whether you're raising that child or made the loving choice to place them with another family—you're still a mom. There's no asterisk on that title.

But motherhood—that conscious, intentional, daily showing up for another human being—that's something that develops. It doesn't always arrive the moment they place a baby in your arms. Sometimes it grows slowly, taking root in the corners of your heart when you least expect it.

Finding My Way to Motherhood

Here's where I'm going to get vulnerable with you in a way that might make some people uncomfortable. I let my first child live with my sister for a while until I could wrap my entire self around the responsibility of being a mother.

I still visited. I still nursed him. He knew I was his mother. But I recognized something crucial: he deserved better than what I could give at that moment, and thank God for a family that truly operates as a village. They stepped in while I worked on becoming the mother he needed.

This decision wasn't wrapped in pretty paper. In a culture that expects maternal love to be immediate and all-consuming, admitting that I wasn't ready felt like wearing a sign that said

"FAILED AT BASIC WOMANHOOD." The judgment—both from others and worse, from myself—was crushing at times.

Was I selfish? Was there something broken in me? Why wasn't I transformed into Mother Teresa the moment I gave birth?

But underneath those doubts was a deeper truth: forcing myself into a role I wasn't emotionally equipped for would have harmed us both. My sister provided a loving, stable environment while maintaining our connection. I still participated in his care, still bonded with him, but with the breathing room I needed to develop emotional resources that weren't magically bestowed upon me in the delivery room.

Looking back, I recognize the courage in that choice. Our culture rarely acknowledges the complexity of maternal emotions, expecting women to seamlessly transform into selfless nurturers regardless of their circumstances, age, or readiness. Choosing an unconventional path required facing criticism, working through my own feelings of inadequacy, and trusting that in the long run, this arrangement would serve my son better than me pretending to be someone I wasn't yet ready to be.

And then the plot twist: turns out, motherhood eventually took to me like a fish to water (hence my eventual eleven children—yes, you read that right). When I finally did embrace motherhood fully, when I reached the point where I could "wrap my entire self around the responsibility," this role that had initially seemed so foreign became as natural as breathing.

This doesn't mean motherhood suddenly became a walk in the unicorn-filled park. It remained challenging, exhausting, and occasionally made me want to lock myself in the bathroom with a secret candy stash (every mom has one, don't lie). But there was a fundamental shift in how I experienced those challenges. What once felt like trying to wear someone else's too-tight shoes became simply part of the rhythm of my days.

Building Our Blended Family

Fast forward to meeting my forever person. I already had children and had built up walls taller than my laundry pile (which is saying something). I was not about to dive into another relationship that would leave me picking up emotional pieces while simultaneously making school lunches.

Turns out, he had children too and wasn't looking to play games. I remember point-blank asking him, "What do you want with me?" His response was simple: "I want you to be my woman."

That, my friends, was the first time I had ever heard those words from a man—direct, clear, no wishy-washy "let's see where this goes" nonsense. So I married him. Along with him came four bonus babies.

In an instant, we became the largest family everywhere we went. Our blended family unit became quite the conversation starter. And by "conversation starter," I mean we became the butt of many jokes.

I can take a joke. I'm funny. I appreciate humor. But sometimes that gets old. Especially when folks ask if you're gonna have anymore or if you're done. Or when your "friends" have a gathering and ask you not to bring your kids. Or they have the gathering and just flat out don't invite you. That gets old faster than bananas on my kitchen counter (which is approximately 2.5 seconds with this many children).

Facing Judgment and Stereotypes

I had to do a lot of deep work to undo the negative perceptions and labels placed on me because of having so many children. The stereotypes. The judgment. And it took time. I used to be ashamed of having so many kids. Then I was ashamed of being ashamed.

The assumptions people make about large families come at you from all angles. The religious assumptions—that we must be following some faith that prohibits birth control. The socioeconomic assumptions—that we must be receiving government assistance or struggling financially. The intelligence assumptions—that we must not understand how reproduction works or lack the foresight to plan our family size.

These stereotypes affected me more deeply than I initially realized. I found myself overcompensating—making sure my children were immaculately dressed in public, highlighting their academic achievements in conversation, NEVER inviting people to our home—all to counter the unspoken judgments I felt directed our way.

My sister jokes (but I think she's serious) about ripping my uterus from my body if I get pregnant again. Sentences in my family jokingly start or end with "With all the kids you got…" Try it yourself! "Where are you going, with all the kids you got?" or "With all the kids you got, you're going out to eat?" It doesn't work all the time, but mostly it does.

Even those closest to us sometimes perpetuate these stereotypes without realizing the impact. The jokes about my fertility, the constant references to our family size as if it's our defining characteristic—they reflect broader cultural discomfort with choices that deviate from the norm.

What these comments miss is the intentionality behind our family size. While not every pregnancy was planned with a

PowerPoint presentation and five-year projections, each child was welcomed, each child was wanted, each child was seen as an addition rather than a burden.

Now, I don't want you to feel sorry for me. I needed to hear all the things I've heard and experience all the things I have. Because that is what has shaped the mother I am today. My children are a huge part of who I am. It is through them that I see my legacy. They give me so much life. Cheer me on when I think I've failed at everything.

I often tell the story about my son Jayce who congratulated me for going to the potty. If my day has gone terribly wrong, and I feel like a complete failure, at least I've done one thing right: going potty. Sometimes the bar is that low, and that's perfectly okay.

The Reality of Motherhood Across Ages and Stages

I have adult children, teens, grade schoolers, and an almost five year old that swears he is as old as the others. At this stage in my life as a mother, I don't ask for advice on parenting and I don't offer any. Wanna know why? Because we're all trying to figure this shit out.

Parenting across such a wide age range gives you perspective that would make a philosopher's head spin. I'm simultaneously helping a young adult navigate college applications while showing my son how to wipe his own butt (ask me how that's going). I'm having conversations about dating and relationships with teenagers while reading bedtime stories to elementary schoolers.

This breadth of experience has shown me that no matter how many children you've raised, each one presents new challenges that make you question everything you thought you knew. Just when you think you've mastered a particular parenting skill, a child comes along who requires a completely different approach.

It's like being a chef who's perfected cooking steaks, only to be handed a live octopus and told "good luck!" Different child, different recipe. Same kitchen, completely different meal.

Back off mom! Ever heard that before?

Never thought I'd hear those words from one of my children. When it comes to parenting, I didn't and still don't have a blueprint. I believe life is the best teacher ever. I loved from the capacity of my heart at the time. I parent with the best intentions and learn from the successes and failures of other parents, namely those who are closest to me—my mother and father, their parents before them.

Those words—*"Back off mom!"*—hit with particular force because they challenge our fundamental understanding of our role as mothers. From the moment they're placed in our arms, we're told that our primary responsibility is protection. Keep them safe. Shield them from harm. Anticipate dangers. Prevent mistakes.

This protective instinct becomes so ingrained that it's hard to recognize when our well-intentioned hovering becomes an impediment rather than a support.

I don't look at manuals written by Pinterest parents who don't have a family like mine or share our culture or beliefs. When I was growing up, I used to tell myself that I would NEVER treat my children like my parents treated me. That was usually when I was in trouble for something completely my fault.

And now here I am nearing my forties with children spanning from toddler to young adult saying and doing some of the things I swore I'd never do. Nitpicking. Yelling. Hovering. Micromanaging my children to the point where they feel they have to tell me to back off.

How did I get here? Am I being #teamtoomuch? Have I turned into another rendition of my parents?

There's a particular cognitive dissonance that occurs when you find yourself repeating the very parenting behaviors you once criticized. The words come out of your mouth—"Because I said so" or "As long as you live under my roof"—and suddenly you hear your mother's voice coming through your lips. It's like a parental out-of-body experience.

Learning When to Let Go

Lately I've been thinking about when to know it's time to let go or to back off, as my son put it. As a mother, I want nothing more than to see my kids grow up safe and successful. It's natural for me to look over them because I've been doing that since I was aware of their existence in my womb.

However, as these children grow up, there's this space—this grey area between being a child and an adult—that I'm not sure I know how to navigate.

Like, do I make them pay rent while also collecting a paycheck? Do they ask permission to leave the house (of course they do)? How do we exchange conversation? Is it one-sided like "do as I say," or two-sided where they can feel free to tell me where I can stick my ideas or suggestions?

I remember when each of them started taking their first steps. I was the literal helicopter mom ensuring a soft landing for each fall. I was there to wipe every tear. And sometimes I helped them walk… well, most of the time I did.

But I found something to be true: the more I tried to help

them walk, the longer it took for them to take off on their own. All of my help was actually hindering their progress. They needed to fall. They needed to learn to balance without me holding their hands.

And so I am still learning the exact timing for letting go. I'm not sure there's a clear-cut answer contrary to Pinterest parent belief. But I can say this one thing: You will know. Your child will know even before you. And it's scary. It hurts to think that they are ready to walk this life out without your hand to hold.

I'm a woman of faith, and I firmly believe that there is someone greater than a helicopter mom on any day. Someone who never slumbers or sleeps. That faith makes it easier for me to relinquish my grip and back off.

I have to trust that my parenting is paying off for my children. That they will be safe and successful. And even if they fall, they can and will get back up. Because it's the falls and failures that help shape us.

So, if your child is urging you to ease up a little, think about it. They might just need that space to grow.

Beyond the Pinterest-Perfect Parenthood

I'm about to drop a bomb on you right now. There isn't a perfect parent out there. All strategies work for the one who has it. Why? Because each child is different and requires something different from you at any moment.

Away with the Pinterest parents who log every milestone on the whitest white background with all the neatly sorted underwear posing perfectly. Seriously. Stop it, and yes, I'm judging. What happens when the baby won't sit still or poops on the white background? What happens when your body won't snap back two weeks after giving birth? The world doesn't need any more Pinterest parents.

We need to see the real. The mama who can't go to the bathroom alone. The one who has the baby hanging from her nipple while she's trying to conduct a meeting. The one who has to gather herself before going into the grocery store because she knows kids are about to go apeshit as soon as the automatic doors open. That's what the world needs to see.

When we present only the polished version of parenthood, we isolate those who are struggling. The mother dealing with postpartum depression looks at those perfect images and concludes that her experience is abnormal. The father overwhelmed by the demands of newborn care believes he's uniquely inadequate. The parents navigating a child's special needs feel additionally burdened by the gap between their reality and the effortless-seeming parenthood portrayed on social media.

A Call for Solidarity Among Mothers

Whether you have one, five, ten, or eleven, I think every experience in motherhood is different. No one has the right to speak on how one mother chooses to parent over another. Mothers should offer a judgment-free zone because our job is hard. Thankless. Unappreciated. Often underestimated and unnoticed.

We have to relabel stay-at-home mom to "domestic engineer" just to get the respect we deserve. Shout out to the moms who instantly became the all-subject teacher for multiple grades, the lunch lady, and guidance counselor during pandemic schooling. Shout out to the one who gave up their career because the job couldn't understand your desire for work/life balance. Shout out to the mom who didn't give up on her dreams and tackled her goals while raising kids, sometimes on her own.

The judgment serves no constructive purpose. It doesn't improve children's outcomes or support maternal wellbeing. If anything, it diverts energy from the real work of parenting into defensive posturing.

What would happen if we approached differences in parenting styles with curiosity rather than judgment? If we recognized that the diversity of approaches reflects not only different personalities but also different children's needs and different family circumstances?

Embracing My Identity as the M.O.M.

My husband is a genius. He comes up with some of the best one-liners out of nowhere, and you wouldn't expect it because his personality isn't a comedian by any means. One day we're sitting down, and he said, "You're the M.O.M. Mother of Many." We both laughed because that's the truth. I have a lot of children. I am literally the mother of many.

And instead of wearing it like a shameful scarlet letter, I decided to add it to the end of my name like a fancy-schmancy title. Trademark pending, so don't even think about it.

This reframing—from "mother of many" as a potential source of embarrassment to "M.O.M." as a title of distinction—represents a significant shift in perspective. It's a reclamation of identity, turning what could be viewed as a liability into a point of pride.

Over the years, I've heard my share of terrible advice. I've second-guessed my parenting skills. I've tried to model my kids after other mothers, but at the end of the day, I can only be me. My family works because the people in it are assigned to me.

We are loud. And I mean you could probably hear us from down the street. We're messy. We're imperfect. We're real. And we're exactly as we should be.

In the end, embracing the reality behind being the M.O.M. isn't about achieving perfection or meeting someone else's standards. It's about finding your unique rhythm, celebrating the chaos alongside the joy, and recognizing that in all your beautiful imperfection, you're exactly the mother your children need you to be.

The Sacred Geography of Home, Heart, and Self

Let me tell you about the night that sent me spiraling down memory lane faster than my kids can find the snacks I've hidden.

There I was, minding my own business, when my daughter walked in with her iPad asking if we could look at Google Earth together. Sure, why not? It seemed innocent enough. My husband joined us, and before I knew it, he was taking control (shocker) and pulling up the house he grew up in.

What started as a casual evening activity turned into this profound journey through time and space that I never saw coming. Isn't that how the most meaningful moments happen? You're just living your regular Tuesday life when—BAM—something cracks your heart wide open.

As he pointed out the tree he climbed after his mama told him not to (boys never change, do they?), the driveway where he learned to ride his bike, and the window of the bedroom he shared with his brother, I saw this whole other person emerge. The boy he was before life shaped him into the man who leaves his socks next to—not in—the hamper. His face softened, his voice changed, and suddenly I was meeting a version of him that only exists in memory.

There's something so vulnerable about showing someone the places that made you. These aren't just buildings or streets—they're the physical containers of who we used to be. When we share them, we're basically saying, "Here's the blueprint of how I became me." That's no small thing.

15 Lambert Drive: Where It All Began
15 Lambert Drive.

I can say those words and instantly I'm transported back to my childhood home. The long driveway where I'd stand during rainstorms, convinced I was drifting away while standing completely still because of how the water flowed around my feet. (Look, I was a dramatic child. Spoiler alert: still am.)

That address is burned into my brain—not just as a location but as a coordinate in my life's timeline. I can still smell the Sunday dinners, hear the specific creak of the third step on the staircase (the one we all learned to skip when sneaking in past curfew), and see exactly how the afternoon light filtered through the living room curtains, making patterns on the carpet that I'd trace with my toes.

But nothing—and I mean NOTHING—stands out in my memories like that plum tree in our yard. Y'all, that tree was EVERYTHING. Every kid in the neighborhood looked at that tree with pure envy, and I felt like royalty because it was in OUR yard. The sidewalk beneath it would turn purple with fallen fruit each summer, marking our property as the coolest spot on the block. The sweet-tart smell of those plums announced to everyone: "This is where the Gaines family lives. This is where I belong."

And then there was Swad, my first boyfriend. Lord have

mercy, was I obsessed! My little heart couldn't handle the intensity of fifth-grade love. I wrote "I love Swad" EVERYWHERE—the back of the couch, inside my closet, in our car, in my aunt's car. Then I'd lie through my teeth when confronted, suggesting maybe my sister did it. Or possibly our dog George, who apparently had both opposable thumbs and romantic feelings for a 10-year-old boy named Swad.

The intensity of that first crush feels ridiculous now, but wasn't it also the purest form of love? There were no complications, no adult expectations—just this overwhelming feeling that made me want to announce it to the world via permanent marker on household furniture. My "relationship" with Swad consisted of exchanging notes in class and occasional awkward phone calls where neither of us knew what to say, yet somehow it felt as significant as any relationship I've had since.

The First Family: Black Excellence Before It Had a Hashtag

15 Lambert Drive wasn't just an address—it was the headquarters of what our community called "the First Family."

If you grew up when and where I did, you understand what this meant. Being part of the First Family wasn't about having the most money or the biggest house. It was about respect. It was about carrying yourself with dignity. It meant your family name opened doors and raised expectations.

We were rich in my eyes. Not Instagram-rich with luxury cars and designer everything, but rich in all the ways that actually mattered to a child. Mom and dad were present. My siblings were my built-in best friends (and occasional worst enemies). I never worried about the basics that made life beautiful.

The truth is, I had no idea if we were financially well-off or just scraping by. Kids have this magical ability to measure "enough" based on what's familiar. As long as there was food on the table, clothes for school, and people who loved me, my wealth-o-meter read "filthy rich." My parents' success wasn't in their bank account but in their ability to shield us from adult worries.

I'm trying to recapture that wisdom with my own kids. In a world that's constantly showing them what they should want next, I want them to feel that same sense of "we have everything we need" that carried me through childhood.

We lived in a thriving Black neighborhood where nothing felt out of place. I never had to code-switch or explain my existence. I felt SAFE—not just physically, but psychologically. I could just BE.

The significance of that environment cannot be overstated. It meant navigating daily life without the constant calculations required in predominantly white spaces. The adults in the neighborhood formed this incredible network of care and accountability. Mrs. Johnson three doors down could absolutely correct you for running in the street, and you bet she'd tell your mama about it later. Mr. Wilson on his porch knew exactly which family you belonged to and what time you should be heading home.

This wasn't surveillance—it was community. It was belonging to something bigger than your individual family.

When Google Earth Shatters the Perfect Picture

So back to our family Google Earth adventure. When I finally looked up my old neighborhood—the place that loomed so large in my memories—I couldn't believe what I saw.

My majestic plum tree? Nothing but a sad little shrub. The neighborhood that felt so spacious and vibrant? Run down and cramped. It has been 30 years, but still, the disconnect between my memory and this reality was jarring.

It's one of life's cruelest tricks—the places that feel enormous and magical in our childhood memories look so ordinary, even diminished, through adult eyes. That dissonance isn't just about physical deterioration over time. It's about the contrast between how we experienced these places as children—when our world was smaller and our capacity for wonder was greater—and how we see them now.

The street that felt like an endless territory for exploration was actually just a short block. The backyard where I created entire fantasy worlds was a modest patch of grass. The plum tree that seemed like it touched the sky was just an average fruit tree.

I didn't need to think too hard to realize that 30 years later, "home" has evolved into something much deeper than an address.

Redefining Home: It's Complicated (And Beautiful)

So what does home mean now? Buckle up, friends, because it's a whole vibe.

Home is a place AND a feeling. It's where my children can be themselves without apology. It's freedom from the fear of eviction notices and uncertainty. It's something that belongs to US—a space we can boldly claim as our own.

Home is where my people are. And by "my people," I mean those I'm related to by blood but also those I've collected along the way—the family I've chosen who love me without conditions or expectations.

Home is where I can take my hair down—or take it ALL off. It's where I can walk around in mismatched socks and my husband's old T-shirt with no makeup and yesterday's twist-out, and nobody bats an eye. It's where I need no apology for simply existing.

Home moves around. It follows love like a loyal pet. It shows up wherever I'm safe to be free and wherever I'm safe to be me.

That means home can be ANYWHERE. It could be in our minivan on a road trip, singing off-key to '90s R&B. It could be sitting beside my husband while he delivers one of his famous "life lectures" that somehow never get shorter no matter how many times he gives them. It's me sitting next to my parents, soaking in their presence while I still can. It's laughing so hard I snort with my sister. It's my grandmother's kitchen, my favorite aunts' hugs, my cousins' inside jokes.

Home is even on Zoom with my girlfriends, who hold my weave when life gets too wild. (Metaphorically speaking, of course, though some of them have literally held my extensions.)

Home is a state of mind—that exhale when you can finally, fully relax. It's being completely connected to yourself and others without performance or pretense.

I can be at home in a crowd of people gathered to hear me speak, feeling that electric connection when a message lands right in their hearts. Home is how people make you feel seen, heard, and valued for exactly who you are.

Home is comfort food—a piece of pound cake with a scoop of ice cream melting on top. It's the first sip of coffee in a quiet house before the kids wake up. It's getting lost in a book that speaks directly to your soul.

It's not being limited by the expectations or judgments of those around you.

You can be in a house and not feel at home. My younger sons always say, "I by myself," when they're in the living room and my husband and I are in our bedroom. Even though we're under the same roof, they need the closeness, the security of being near us to truly feel at home.

Home is where hearty, loud laughter bounces off the walls. It's the familiar scent that greets you when you walk through the door after being away—that smell that whispers, "Hello, welcome back to where you belong."

Home is looking up at the clouds and feeling small in the best possible way. It's the warmth of sunshine on your skin. It's knowing you have somewhere you can always return to, even if that somewhere is just the quiet center of your own heart.

I realize now why I didn't recognize my childhood neighborhood on Google Earth. It's no longer my home. It belongs to someone else now, just as where I currently live used to be someone else's home. The physical spaces we inhabit are just temporary containers for the real home that travels with us wherever we go—because home is where the heart lives.

The People Who Make a House a Home

Let's talk about family, shall we? Sometimes it's the blood that binds. But then again, you can share DNA with someone and still feel like complete strangers.

Family is so much more than your biological relatives. The bonds we form with our hearts can be just as strong—sometimes stronger—than those formed in the womb.

Some of the closest humans to my heart share zero genetic material with me. We picked each other. These are the friends who have seen me at my absolute worst and somehow still answer my texts. The ones who hold my weave, girl. The ones who know exactly when to bring coffee and when to bring wine. The bonus parents who speak life into my children.

The relationships that spill over into family are those that require no explanation. They just ARE. When I get together with my found family, it's unplanned and effortless. We just show up for each other. If one of us is hurting, no formal invitation needs to be sent—we're just there, tissues and chocolate in hand.

We might fight and hold a spectacular grudge (I'm working on this in therapy, okay?), but let someone from the outside come for one of us? It's ON. Like, I can complain about my sister all day long, but if you say ONE word against her, I will transform into her fiercest defender faster than you can say "family loyalty."

These are the people I can be 100% myself with—pull my weave out, kick off my shoes, show up with no makeup on, ugly cry until mascara runs down my face. Do just about anything with and know I'm still loved.

Pro tip though: Family and business don't mix well. If I can fall up in your place unannounced at midnight, barefoot and bra-less, with zero questions asked, that comfortable boundary-blurring doesn't translate well to professional settings. Trust me on this one.

The Blood Bonds: Wonderfully Imperfect

My blood family is this beautiful, dysfunctional, loving, solid unit. Debra and Ronnie are my beginning—they chose to make me, keep me, raise me. They messed up sometimes (haven't we all?), but they loved consistently.

Angel, Joshua, Bethany, and Terrence are my siblings. Angel is the oldest, but because I'm taller, people think she's younger than me. This drives me absolutely INSANE, which she finds hilarious. My brother Josh is a giant, but he's younger than me. I used to tattle on him for breathing—literally BREATHING—because I was that petty. But today he's one of my best friends.

Bethany is the baby in every sense of the word. She can do no wrong, and to this day, my parents will drop everything to see about her. Baby sibling perks that I'm still slightly bitter about, to be honest.

Terrance, God rest his soul, was my oldest brother. I remember him as the sweet one, always smiling, never letting anyone know if something was wrong.

Grandma Hattie Lou, my mom's mama, lives in Arkansas. She used to call me her "heart baby," which made me feel like the chosen one (don't tell my siblings). She's taught me more about love and hard work than anyone else. She loves God with such intensity that if anyone should be taken up to heaven without dying like Enoch in the Bible, it should be Grandma Hattie.

Summers with Granny meant FREEDOM. All us cousins would pile into her bed, giggling and squirming until she'd start reading Bible stories. Some days we'd stay home with Uncle Eric watching daytime TV like we were grown—The Price is Right, followed by a soap opera marathon that if you know, you know. Starting with Young and the Restless, Days of Our Lives, All My Children, and General Hospital. And I know there were more but if I didn't mention it, we didn't watch it, honey. We'd drink Kool-Aid that was always too sweet but somehow perfect; I'm talking about the red and purple kind.

The penny store was our wonderland. We'd count our coins with the seriousness of Wall Street bankers, making sure we got the maximum candy possible. And those Arkansas highways seemed to stretch forever, promising adventures at places like DeGray Lake.

I can still see Granny fishing with endless patience. She'd bring those fish home, gut and clean them right in the kitchen, wasting nothing. We'd have the freshest fish dinner that night, feeling like royalty.

Remember Ramen noodles before they were trendy? And putting foil on the TV antenna to catch our favorite shows? We'd sing En Vogue at the top of our lungs, convinced we sounded exactly like them.

My ashy legs would kick up dust on those unpaved roads. Sometimes we'd come home with ticks, and Granny would give us alcohol baths that stung like crazy but did the job.

Church meant hardwood floors that announced your arrival with every step. White folded socks, Vaseline on our knees so the ash wouldn't show. Those choir robes, marching in like soldiers for the Lord. Getting in trouble from the pulpit was THE WORST—your name called out for everyone to hear. But the dinners in the church basement made up for it.

That was home to me.

Moving to the Midwest changed everything—my footing, my belonging, my sense of place. At 42, I'm still trying to reconnect with those roots. I'm here, but I know I'm not FROM here.

My Partner, My Home

My husband is a huge part of my definition of home. He sometimes raises an eyebrow at my wild ideas, but he's super supportive of my continuous transformation. And THAT, my friends, is why I'm grateful for him.

The way he encourages me, the way he sits with me to help me see through projects no matter how ridiculous they seemed at first—it's something special. I guess he's used to me not having your everyday kind of ideas. So even when he visibly cringes at their mention, he stays through with me until they're completed. And he doesn't just stay; he participates in whatever way he can.

My husband should really be the one writing a book. The man is a TALKER. Sometimes living with him feels like being at a never-ending TED Talk. He always seems to have a compelling line or two in his lectures to the kids. Short speeches are not his thing, though. He talks LONG. He tells the same stories with as much passion as the first time, and I somehow forget I've heard them before until something tips me off. While I hear these stories on repeat, the world should hear them too—but that's his journey, his choice to make.

He has always encouraged me. He told me I could cook even when I was baking hot dogs and microwaving spaghetti. (To be clear: that is NOT cooking. That is survival.) He has always supported me, always been sure to tell me I'm doing well. He boosts me with his words.

I'm finally in a faithful relationship. No man outside of my dad has ever treated me like a queen until him. No man has ever made me feel so special. I opened up about everything in my life, and he never judged me. He embraced me—past, present, and all my messy bits.

That's real. That's rare.

He called me his virtuous woman even when I felt like I'd lost all virtue. He saw greatness in me when I couldn't see it in the mirror. He saw value when I felt worthless. He saw beauty when I felt ugly inside and out.

I'm not battered anymore. I'm not afraid anymore. I'm not confused anymore. I'm not assaulted anymore. I'm not insecure anymore.

I am in a safe and healthy relationship.

What. A. Gift.

My Hair Journey = My Life Journey

My hair has gone through more transformations than a Hollywood actress trying to stay relevant. The earliest style I remember was the three-part plaits—the top two braided together and sealed with a white barrette, with the plait in the back hanging just above my shoulders.

Then there was the Jheri curl era. My mother had been doing a wave nouveau and decided her daughters needed to join the moisture-rich craze. Many-a car window and wall fell victim to my Care Free Curl residue. That grease stain doesn't come out, y'all. It only smears.

I was BEYOND grateful to move on from the curl to braids. Everyone had them in the nineties. I had dookie braids—thick synthetic extensions that made me feel like Lisa Bonet. Then I graduated to a relaxer. To have straight hair without a hot comb was revolutionary! The only downside was the burning sensation that came when I inevitably scratched my scalp the night before, despite Mom's warnings. The chemical burns never deterred us from going back every few weeks for a touch-up. Beauty is pain, right? (Wrong, but that's what we believed.)

Then my sister got the grand idea that she could be a hairdresser. I was her first client. Who else would volunteer? She gave my tresses what I'll generously call an "asymmetrical bob looking thing." I put the HOT in hot mess. From then on, I kept variations of the short look out of necessity—finger waves, crimps, the mushroom cut, flips, cornrows. I made the most of my sister's "creative expression."

As I got older, my hairstyles became more aligned with my inner state. They were expressions of what was happening on the inside. New relationship? New hairstyle. New job? New hairstyle. Going through a tough season? Off with all my hair! I've literally cut it all off multiple times. Wigs became my best friend. I would glue them, sew them, or crochet them— whatever the situation called for.

My hairstyles are ever-evolving—just like me. I remember as a kid, I couldn't WAIT to be a teenager. Then, as a teen, I couldn't wait to be twenty-one. Now I'm 42 - carrying 40 with all the wisdom and battle scars that come with it - as one of my kids so helpfully reminds me. My check engine light is permanently on, and some days I'm clinging to my youth like it's the last slice of pizza at a sleepover.

Let me tell you something I wish someone had convinced me to believe when I was younger: rushing to be an adult is NOT the move. At all. Right now, I would happily trade places with a five-year-old for nap time and ready-made meals versus things like RESPONSIBILITIES. I don't know the clinical term for ignoring good advice when you're young, but I definitely had a severe case. I'm sure my parents tried to tell me to enjoy my youth. I didn't listen. I didn't care.

Now I tell my kids the same thing, and guess what? They don't listen either. The circle of life continues.

We should learn to enjoy every moment where we find ourselves. As much as possible. I didn't regret any hairstyle I chose—at least not while I was wearing it. I rocked them all with confidence (even my sister's disaster cut). Each style made me feel something specific for that phase of life.

We must learn to bask in whatever season we're in. Not to stay there forever, but not to rush to the next thing before we've fully experienced the present. There's no time like today to enjoy today.

I think the way my hairstyles evolved mirrors how life evolves. Life is meant to be progressive. You're not meant to be a child forever. Things shift. Things get upgraded. Things improve. We're not expected to stay in one spot.

We evolve. Just like my hair, just like my understanding of home, just like my definition of family—always changing, always growing, always becoming more authentically me.

Finding Purpose in Life's Ministry

Let me tell you about the time I thought I was destined to be the next great female evangelist. I'm talking full-on, hands laid, people-falling-out kind of ministry. Powerful. Dynamic. The whole shebang.

I would have these dreams—vivid, technicolor visions of standing in front of massive crowds hanging on my every word. In my dreams, I'd touch someone's forehead and *boom*—they'd be slain in the spirit, transformed by the power flowing through me. I'd wake up convinced these weren't just random dreams but divine previews of my future.

And why wouldn't I think that? I grew up in church. Not just Sunday-best, Christmas-and-Easter church, but immersed-in-every-service, multiple-times-a-week church. I watched powerhouse preachers command rooms, saw how people responded to a well-delivered sermon with tears and shouts and visible transformation. From my little-girl perspective, the pulpit looked like the pinnacle of purpose.

Plus, it was the family business. My brother? That man is a PREACHER with all caps. From the opening scripture to the altar call, he has it down to a science. My dad and uncle too—I grew up watching them preach with authority and conviction. These were my models, my blueprints for what ministry looked like.

So when I finally got my shot, my chance to step behind that pulpit and deliver the message burning in my heart...

Well, let's just say reality came at me fast.

Between being nervous, having too many notes, and watching the clock tick down my allotted time, I'd give myself a solid 4 out of 10. I brought some good nuggets—don't get me wrong—but it wasn't the earth-shattering, heaven-opening experience I'd imagined.

The disconnect was jarring. Where was the power I'd felt in my dreams? Where was the natural flow, the divine download, the congregation hanging on my every word?

Here's what I finally realized after too many attempts to recreate something that wasn't authentically mine: I was trying to be someone else. I was measuring my effectiveness, my calling, my entire ministry by someone else's blueprint.

And that's a thing we do, isn't it?

We get so caught up in who others are that appeal to us. We try to force ourselves into molds that weren't designed for our unique shape. We forget that we are special in our own mind-blowing way. Like, literally—no one is like me! I am that special something the world has been waiting for. That extra. I am one big, irreplaceable piece in the puzzle called life. The world can't afford for me to go missing because I forgot to be myself.

The same is true for you, by the way. You're not the backup dancer in someone else's music video. You're the star of your own show.

Permission to Be Authentically You

Several years later, I finally know who I am. And a theatrical shouting dancing yelling creature is who I am NOT.

My great grandfather, Rev. E. R. Gaines, used to say something that would make English teachers everywhere cringe but contains more wisdom than most fancy philosophy books: "Be who you is and not who you ain't. Cuz if you ain't who you is, you is who you ain't."

I know—it takes a minute to untangle that pretzel of pronouns. But once you get it, you GET IT.

When I try to be someone I'm not—when I try to preach like my brother or speak with my father's cadence or build my ministry around someone else's gifts—I'm not just failing at being them (because, duh, I'm not them). I'm also failing at being ME. And that's the real tragedy.

Because while the world has seen plenty of powerful pulpit preachers, it has never—not once in the history of humanity—seen YOUR specific combination of gifts, experiences, perspective, and purpose. Your unique ministry. Your authentic voice.

Finding that voice isn't usually a lightning-bolt moment. For most of us, it's more like archaeological work—carefully brushing away the layers of "should" and "supposed to" until we uncover what's been there all along.

For me, the excavation happened through paying attention to when I felt most alive, most connected, most effective in communicating truth. It wasn't in formal sermon delivery but in conversations. In writing. In smaller group settings where I could be responsive and relational.

My gift wasn't oratorical fireworks but something quieter yet no less powerful—the ability to break down complex spiritual concepts into language people could actually understand.

To create spaces where people felt safe enough to be honest. To listen deeply and respond thoughtfully.

Turns out, I wasn't called to stand behind a traditional pulpit at all.

I was called to create new ones.

Your Life is the Pulpit

And so now I preach. With my life. With my experiences.

My pulpit might be on a podcast, YouTube, the news, Instagram live, or Facebook. It might be a keynote at a conference or sitting on a panel. I'm not limited to a building and platform. My sermon comes in written form as well as spoken. It happens when I lean in to really listen to someone who needs to be heard.

Whether it's lecturing at a university or speaking at a graduation for non-traditional students, my message is about faith, failure, and purpose—themes that translate across contexts and audiences.

This expanded understanding of ministry isn't a consolation prize or a backup plan. It's an evolution—a more nuanced and contemporary expression of the same calling that has animated spiritual leaders throughout history.

Think about it: Jesus himself rarely limited his teaching to the synagogues. Some of his most powerful moments happened on hillsides, from boats, around dinner tables, during walks between towns. He used the communication tools that worked for his context: stories drawn from everyday life, one-on-one conversations, object lessons from nature.

Today's digital landscape offers unprecedented opportunities for this kind of boundary-crossing communication. A thoughtful Instagram post might reach someone who would never enter a church building. A podcast conversation might touch hearts that remain closed to traditional sermons.

And let's be real—living your message is a much higher bar than just speaking it once a week. It's far easier to craft a compelling 30-minute sermon than to embody those principles consistently in how you parent, how you handle conflict, how you manage money, how you treat the barista who messed up your order.

But it's precisely this integration of message and messenger that creates the most profound impact. People may debate theology all day long, but they can't easily dismiss the evidence of a life visibly transformed by the principles you're promoting.

When Your Mess Becomes Your Message

My gift to this world is inspiration, because when you come to your last hope and don't see how you'll make it through, I want you to think about me. Think about my story. Think about all I've had to go through.

Think about every experience that shaped me. Every encounter. Every setback that pushed me back down and every force that pushed me back up. Trust me, I have fallen a LOT. But guess what? I rose again each time.

I want you to think about how I rose each time. Think about the disappointments I had to swallow. The pain I endured. The stigma I faced from the time I was a little girl.

Think about the prices I've paid. The lies told to me and about me. How I was taken advantage of. How I was bruised. Wounded. Abused.

Think about how I sucked it all in and kept going. I was laughed at, underestimated, misunderstood, left out, rejected. So many times I wanted to give up. I believed I wasn't worth it.

Felt unloved. I have my share of scars—visible and invisible.

I'm not sharing this to make you feel sorry for me. (Please don't. Awkward.) I'm sharing because there's unique power in personal testimony—in a first-hand account of struggle, resilience, and transformation that theory alone can never match.

When I share my journey not as a polished success story but as an honest narrative of stumbles and recoveries, failures and comebacks, I create space for you to recognize your own struggles and imagine your own possibilities.

It's not about me saying "look how special I am" but "look what's possible for all of us." The focus isn't on me as an individual but on the principles my story illustrates: resilience isn't magical but methodical. Transformation isn't instantaneous but incremental. Purpose emerges not despite our challenges but often because of them.

There's something incredibly freeing about hearing someone else name the wounds you've experienced too. It creates permission for you to acknowledge yours without shame. It normalizes the struggle and validates the pain while simultaneously showing that these experiences don't have to define your future.

Finding Strength in Vulnerability (Yes, Really)

Sometimes my little ones will cry when I wake them in the mornings. I tell them, "Listen, if I don't cry when I wake up in the morning, no one should. I've had too many legit reasons to. But I still don't."

That's because I've found I am stronger than even my wild mind can ever imagine.

This isn't just a cute mom moment. It contains a profound

truth about resilience and perspective. Without minimizing my children's feelings, I'm gently contextualizing them. Yes, getting up early feels hard. And also, we humans can handle hard things.

I'm not denying my painful past when I say, "I've had too many legit reasons to cry." I'm acknowledging it directly while simultaneously demonstrating that those experiences don't determine my present responses or future possibilities.

When I say, "But I still don't," I'm not suggesting that crying is wrong or that feelings should be suppressed. I'm showing that while I cannot control all my circumstances, I retain significant power over my responses to them.

Healing isn't about erasing painful histories but about developing new relationships to them—not being controlled by past wounds even as we acknowledge their reality.

And here's the kicker: I've discovered I'm stronger than even my wildest imagination could have predicted. Often our most restrictive boundaries aren't external but internal—the stories we tell ourselves about what we can endure, what we can overcome, what we can become.

True strength isn't the absence of vulnerability but the courage to acknowledge it while refusing to be limited by it. It's recognizing both our wounds and our capacity to heal from them, both our fears and our ability to act despite them.

Resilience isn't a fixed trait we either have or lack. It's a skill we develop through consistent practice—choosing to get up one more time than we fall, choosing to begin again despite knowing we may fail again.

The Full Picture: Joy After Pain

But here's what I need you to understand: A testimony that

only talks about the hard stuff isn't complete.

That's why I'm saying to you now that above and beyond all of these challenges, you should think about my victories. Think about my joys. Think about my laughter, full and warm. Think about my strengths.

Think about my drive to be, to do, to achieve, to act, to push, to become, to function, to not just survive but to THRIVE, to excel, to LIVE!

There's a crucial difference between surviving and thriving. Surviving means enduring hardship without being destroyed by it—continuing to function, maintaining basic stability, getting through each day.

Thriving means moving beyond mere endurance to growth, creativity, and flourishing—not just withstanding challenges but being strengthened through them, not just continuing to exist but expanding in capacity and contribution.

When survival consumes all available energy and resources, thriving can seem like an unattainable luxury. I get that. There have been seasons where just making it through the day took everything I had.

But I need you to know that movement from survival to thriving is possible. Others have made this journey despite daunting obstacles. Your current circumstances, however difficult, don't represent your permanent limitation or ultimate destination.

Think about how full and saturated my life has become that I now am able to share from the overflow. Think about the joys of family. Think about how I found shoulders to lean on, to cry on, to simply squeeze. Think about the joys of friends. Think about the joys of having people… someone around so that I am simply never alone.

Think about the joys of life! Think about love that heals.

This shift from individual resilience to relational resources acknowledges that healing and growth happen not in isolation but in community. Being "so full and saturated" that I can "share from the overflow" isn't just poetic language; it's practical wisdom about sustainable giving. We can only consistently offer to others what we've first received ourselves.

This isn't selfishness but stewardship—recognizing that maintaining our own wellbeing isn't separate from serving others but essential to it.

Sometimes we need practical assistance (shoulders to lean on), sometimes emotional space (shoulders to cry on), and sometimes simple human connection (shoulders to squeeze). Each form of support matters; none can fully substitute for the others.

And that phrase "so that I am simply never alone" speaks to one of our deepest human fears and most fundamental needs. Isolation magnifies suffering, while connection—even when it cannot remove our pain—provides crucial context and comfort for enduring it.

This healing doesn't erase all scars or eliminate all struggles, but it creates new possibilities beyond them—new narratives, new connections, new futures not determined by past wounds.

Your Life is Speaking (Make Sure It's Saying Something Good)

I think about the words I spoke to myself that brought me out of some dark moments. My stories are sometimes unpleasant, but they don't end in misery and loss. They are beautiful.

There is so much strength that has emerged from the

weaknesses I've learned from. All of this helped me find purpose. Everything that happened to me was interconnected and meant to mold me.

I didn't break.

My life speaks. It preaches. It helps others, and that is good preaching.

The internal narratives we construct and repeat shape our perception of both our circumstances and our capacities. In dark moments, the ability to speak truth to ourselves—to counter despair with hope, limitation with possibility, isolation with connection—can make the difference between surrender and perseverance.

This isn't magical thinking but intentional reframing that creates space for new perspectives and possibilities.

When I acknowledge that "my stories are sometimes unpleasant," I'm maintaining unflinching honesty while insisting that difficult beginnings don't determine endings. This balanced perspective avoids both the trap of toxic positivity (denying the reality of suffering) and the trap of defining identity primarily through trauma (allowing past pain to become the dominant narrative).

Instead, it places hardship within a larger context of growth, meaning, and beauty that emerges not despite suffering but often through it.

Finding "so much strength from the weaknesses I have learned from" echoes the paradoxical wisdom found in many spiritual traditions: that vulnerability can become a source of power, limitation a source of insight, brokenness a source of connection.

This isn't romanticizing suffering but recognizing its potential transformative value when processed within supportive contexts and constructive frameworks. Our areas of greatest pain, when healed and integrated, often become our areas of greatest contribution.

Seeing everything as "interconnected and meant to mold me" offers a framework for finding meaning in even the most difficult experiences. This isn't suggesting that suffering is orchestrated for our benefit. Rather, it's recognizing how even random or malicious events can be incorporated into our growth when approached with resilience and supported by community.

It's not that everything happens for a reason, but that we can find purpose within everything that happens.

"I didn't break" affirms both the severity of the challenges faced and the sufficiency of the resources brought to bear against them. It acknowledges both vulnerability (the real possibility of breaking) and strength (the actual outcome of remaining intact).

And finally, "My life speaks. It preaches. It helps others and that is good preaching" brings us full circle to where we started. What began as a constrained understanding focused on traditional pulpit preaching has evolved into an expansive vision where life itself becomes the primary medium of message.

This isn't abandoning the call to ministry but fulfilling it more authentically and effectively through alignment of word and deed, profession and practice, formal communication and lived example.

When our lives visibly demonstrate the principles we espouse, our words gain credibility and power beyond what they could achieve in isolation. This isn't performance or pretense but authentic alignment—becoming in reality what we call others to become, embodying the transformation we invite others to experience.

It's ministry not just as profession but as identity, not just as discrete activity but as holistic expression.

So let me ask you: What is your life preaching right now? What message are others receiving from how you live, how you love, how you respond to both blessings and challenges?

You don't need a pulpit or a platform, a title or a degree. You just need the courage to be authentically yourself—to embrace your unique calling, to share your particular story, to offer your specific gifts without apology or pretense.

Because the world doesn't need another carbon copy of someone else's ministry. It needs the ministry that only you can provide. The testimony that only you can share. The healing that can flow uniquely through your particular combination of wounds and wisdom.

You are that special something the world has been waiting for. Stop hiding. Stop comparing. Stop trying to be who you ain't.

Be who you is. The world is waiting.

From My Journey Back to Yours

My dear friends, as I write these final pages, I feel like we've been on a long road trip together—sharing stories, passing snacks, and occasionally taking wrong turns that somehow led us exactly where we needed to be. Now we're nearing that moment where we pull into your driveway, but before you step out of the car, there's something important I need to say.

The Beautiful Mess That Makes Us Whole

Would you believe that I'm finally making peace with my flaws? Those half-written pages, broken commitments, and spectacular failures I once tried to hide have turned out to be the very ingredients that make me... well, *me*.

And you know what? The same is true for you.

Throughout these chapters, I've invited you into corners of my life that I once kept locked up tight. You've seen me at my best and my absolute messiest. And now, coming full circle, I understand something I wish I'd known years ago: We're not who we are *despite* our experiences, but *because* of them.

For so long, I thought growth meant fixing all my flaws, sanding down my rough edges until I was smooth and perfect. I thought I needed to edit out the messy parts until only the "good" remained. As if life were some kind of spiritual plastic surgery that would eventually turn me into someone worthy of love and belonging.

But that's not how transformation works. Real change isn't about erasing our weaknesses—it's about integrating all parts of ourselves into a beautiful, complicated whole. It's like making a mosaic from broken pieces—the cracks don't disappear; they become essential to the art.

My strengths make me who I am. My failures make me who I am. My weird quirks and inconsistencies make me who I am. And your journey, while uniquely yours, follows this same pattern. We are all walking collections of triumphs, disasters, and everyday in-betweens that somehow add up to something quite extraordinary.

When Sharing Your Truth Feels Terrifying

Can I tell you a secret? Choosing to write this book scared me to death.

For years, I kept these stories to myself, convinced they were either too personal, too painful, or too insignificant to matter to anyone else. Writing meant facing not just the memories themselves, but the fear of how you might judge me for them.

Would you think less of me for my mistakes? Question my credibility because of my failures? Dismiss my insights because I'm still very much a work in progress with a to-do list longer than CVS receipts?

These questions haunted me as I wrote, sometimes sending me straight to the pantry for emotional support cookies. (Don't judge—we all have our coping mechanisms, and mine happen to involve chocolate chips.)

What finally pushed me forward wasn't courage—it was

necessity. I realized I don't need everyone to understand or agree with me. My story doesn't need universal validation to be real. What matters is that I've done the work to process these experiences, learn from them, and perhaps—just perhaps—they might help someone else feel less alone.

The prayers I whispered weren't about success or recognition. They came from a deep desire to ensure my struggles weren't just for me—that maybe the wisdom that cost me so much could light someone else's path, even just a little bit.

If sharing my journey makes your road even slightly easier, then everything I went through carries greater meaning. That's the beautiful alchemy of vulnerability—it transforms personal pain into collective healing.

The Home You've Been Searching For

The most transformative discovery of my entire journey can be summed up in one sentence: What I spent years searching for outside myself was waiting inside me all along.

This isn't some cheesy self-help platitude. It's the hard-won truth that fundamentally changed everything for me.

The belonging I desperately sought in groups, organizations, and relationships mattered, yes. But it remained incomplete until I first belonged to myself—until I claimed my own experience, honored my own truth, and accepted my own complexity without conditions.

It's like the difference between renting and owning your sense of self—one can be taken away at any moment; the other is yours no matter what happens around you. External validation feels amazing (and who doesn't want a good compliment?), but building your entire sense of worth on it is like constructing a house on sand when solid ground is available.

Learning to speak to myself with the same compassion I'd offer a beloved friend wasn't self-indulgence—it was survival. The kindness I'd readily extend to everyone else but systematically deny myself wasn't just ironic, it was unsustainable.

The Courage to Look Inward

Writing this book evolved into something far more profound than I initially imagined. What started as sharing insights became a fundamental reckoning with who I am, how I became this person, and who I might yet become.

It was like cleaning out the garage after ten years of shoving things inside and slamming the door—I knew it would be messy, but I had no idea how emotional I'd get finding my child's first pair of shoes in a dusty box I thought contained Christmas decorations.

Facing my fears meant examining not just what frightens me but why these particular fears have held such power. Admitting weaknesses required moving beyond both denial ("I don't have that problem") and defensiveness ("Yes, but only because...").

The hardest part? Giving voice to my strengths. Years of conditioning against "bragging" had left me reflexively dismissing compliments and minimizing achievements. Learning to recognize and claim my strengths—not as points of superiority but as authentic aspects of who I am—required deliberate practice and a willingness to feel uncomfortable.

It's about sweeping out all the dirt from under the carpet of my soul and acknowledging what has hurt me, defeated me, disappointed me. Conceding that abuse took chunks of me away and I let it. Then, finding the courage to heal those old wounds instead of just covering them up with busy-ness and false positivity.

Beyond the Band-Aid Approach to Healing

Let's be real about something: We live in a culture obsessed with toxic positivity—that insistence that we focus exclusively on the bright side, that we "get over" painful experiences through determination alone.

It's like telling someone with a broken leg to just think positive thoughts and run a marathon. Not helpful, potentially harmful, and definitely annoying.

You can't heal what you won't feel, my friend.

Acknowledging what hurt me meant revisiting moments of injury without rushing toward premature closure. Removing the blinds over deception meant recognizing the ways I had sometimes been complicit in my own suffering—not to blame myself but to reclaim my power going forward.

It's like finally admitting you're lost and checking the map instead of driving in circles insisting you know exactly where you're going. (Not that I've ever done that. Much.)

There's something painfully refreshing about ripping off the Band-Aid and allowing the bitter air of truth to hit our wounds. That momentary sting that precedes relief, the exposure that precedes integration, the vulnerability that precedes strength—this is the paradoxical nature of real healing.

From My Heart to Yours

I'm not sharing my path as a template for you to follow. I'm not handing you a map with X marking the spot where happiness lives. I'm simply walking beside you for a while, pointing out some landmarks I recognized along the way, in case they help you navigate your own unique terrain.

The comfort of not being alone shouldn't be underestimated. So much of human suffering is intensified by isolation—the belief that our struggles are uniquely shameful, that others would reject us if they knew our full truth.

Breaking this isolation creates space for authentic connection based not on curated presentations of perfection but on mutual recognition of our shared humanity. It's like finally taking off the Spanx of the soul—exhaling into the relief of being fully seen and accepted.

My hope is that something in these pages might:

Push you to get up from that ground where you've laid for so long in surrender

Give you strength to take one more step when you feel like quitting

Help you realize you're closer to the light at the end of the tunnel than you think

Offer practical solutions through seeing patterns in my experience that mirror your own

The Magic of Small Steps

Transformation rarely happens through dramatic lightning-bolt moments. Real change begins with small shifts—a slight change in perspective, a modest adjustment in daily practice, a tentative experiment with new responses.

The strength to take that first step often comes not from extraordinary courage but from the simple realization that remaining still has become more painful than moving forward. It's like finally acknowledging that the rock in your shoe is actually bothering you enough to stop and take it out.

So many people abandon their healing journey just before

breakthrough, not because they lack capacity but because they lack perspective. They can't see how far they've come or how close they are to meaningful transformation.

The Power of Specific Stories

I'm telling these stories because I believe they will help someone specific:

Someone who feels afraid but needs to act anyway. Someone struggling to rise above abuse and reclaim their power. Someone who was bullied and still hears those voices louder than their own. Someone carrying scars that haven't fully healed. Someone who was never given permission to speak their truth. Someone who pleases everyone but themselves.

When you're stuck in fear, a lecture on courage isn't helpful. What resonates is hearing from someone who faced similar fears and found a way forward anyway. Their experience doesn't just inspire—it gives you something tangible to hold onto when theory isn't enough.

Overcoming abuse requires rebuilding not just your life but your fundamental sense of self, learning to trust again, and recognizing what healthy relationships actually look like. Hearing from others who've walked this road shows you that healing, while not linear, is genuinely possible.

For people-pleasers (like I used to be), years of accommodating everyone else makes identifying your own needs nearly impossible. You become so focused on keeping peace that your own desires fade into background noise. Hearing someone say, "Your needs matter too," can be the permission you've been waiting for to finally listen to yourself.

The Beautiful Complexity of Being Human

Here's a truth I wish someone had told me earlier: Shedding tears doesn't make you weak. Sometimes I feel fragile, broken, and completely incapable—a beginner at things I thought I'd mastered long ago. These moments come and go like waves, and that's perfectly normal.

Our emotional landscapes aren't meant to be static. The expectation of constant stability is not only unrealistic but unhealthy. Resilience isn't about eliminating these waves but learning to ride them with more grace.

Denying my feelings only led to their eventual eruption in much more destructive ways. It's like trying to hold a beach ball underwater—you can manage it for a while, but eventually, it's going to pop up with force, probably smacking you in the face in the process.

So I've learned to face my emotions. Own them. I know I'm irrational sometimes. Short-tempered sometimes. And that's okay—it's part of being human. Accepting this doesn't mean I stop growing; it means I grow from a place of truth rather than pretense.

Finding Strength in Weakness

I've discovered something that changed everything: I can be fearful and still have courage. I can be uncertain and still move forward. I can be imperfect and still be exactly who I'm meant to be.

Remembering that "God's strength is made perfect in weakness" (II Corinthians 12:9) revolutionized my understanding of my own limitations. Rather than viewing weakness as an obstacle to divine work, I now see it creates optimal conditions for grace to operate. My inadequacy becomes not a barrier but an invitation to experience strength beyond my own resources.

The most beautiful things happen in my life when I don't have it all together. When I don't have it all figured out. When I don't feel strong enough or even good enough.

It's like admitting I don't know how to bake a cake, and suddenly finding myself working alongside a master pastry chef who guides my hands—my limitations become the entry point for something I could never create alone.

What Matters Most

With so much life behind me (and still ahead), I had to ask myself: What can I leave in this world if this were my first and only chance? What truly matters among all my experiences?

As much as I'd love to tell you about the chaos and joy of raising 11 children, or how I discovered my passion for baking, or share my favorite childhood memories, I needed to go deeper and search for the essence—the truth that might serve others most.

This decision reflects both intention about legacy and discernment about what matters most. It's like packing for a journey with limited space—you bring what will serve the greatest purpose, what might light someone else's way when the path gets dark.

Coming Full Circle

As we reach the end of our time together, I return to where we began—with you. Everything I've shared about my journey ultimately serves one purpose: to illuminate possibilities for your own path forward.

My story matters because it might help you recognize the significance of yours. My healing matters because it might create space for yours. My truth matters because it might embolden you to claim yours.

In recognizing parts of yourself in my struggles, you might glimpse your potential in my becoming. In witnessing my imperfect but persistent journey toward wholeness, you might find courage for your own next steps.

Whatever brought you to these pages—curiosity, recommendation, random chance, or deliberate seeking—I believe there's purpose in our paths crossing through these words. Perhaps something specific I've shared will unlock a door you've been trying to open. Perhaps knowing someone else has navigated similar territory will provide the assurance you need to continue your unique exploration.

As you close this book and continue your own story, remember this: you carry within you everything essential for your journey. The belonging, acceptance, affirmation, and motivation you seek externally exist already within you, waiting to be recognized and claimed.

This doesn't mean you don't need others—we all require community and loving connection. But these external resources complement rather than create your fundamental capacity for growth, healing, and purposeful living.

Your story matters. Your struggles matter. Your insights matter. Your becoming matters. The world needs the unique gift that only you can offer—not some idealized version of yourself free from flaws and limitations, but the actual, complex, gloriously human you that exists right now, with all your contradictions, challenges, and extraordinary potential.

The journey back to yourself has already begun.

Keep going.

With boundless hope and faith in you,

Your fellow traveler on this messy, beautiful road

Acknowledgments

First and always, **God**—Your grace sustains me, Your wisdom guides me, and Your love carries me through every season. Without You, none of this would be possible.

To my **husband and life partner, Brent Fox**—you already know. But in case you forgot, thank you for being my anchor, my encourager, and my soft place to land. I love you endlessly.

To **Brandi Bothe**, your creative vision brought this cover to life in a way that speaks volumes. Thank you for capturing the essence of this book with such artistry.

To **Joshua Foo**, your unmatched photography elevated this new edition beyond what I imagined. Your gift is undeniable, and I'm grateful to have your talent as part of this journey.

To my **children**, who were my behind-the-scenes team—your patience, your little feet padding around when the nights stretched long, and your love kept me going. You may not have held the pen, but you held me up.

And to **you, the reader**—thank you for walking this journey with me. Your willingness to reflect, grow, and embrace your own story makes every word worth writing.

Any typos? Blame this first—but not last—solo effort and labor of love.

With love and gratitude,
Rachel D. Fox

About the Author

Rachel D. Fox is a speaker, author, and transformational coach dedicated to helping others reclaim their power and walk boldly in their purpose. With a passion for faith, personal growth, and leadership, she blends wisdom, humor, and real-life experience to inspire people from all walks of life.

As the founder of **Catapult Consulting Solutions** and **Flourish Coaching & Consulting**, Rachel empowers individuals and organizations to break barriers, lead with confidence, and embrace transformation. Her work has been recognized in **Omaha Magazine, the Inspire Awards, and the TOYO Awards**, and she has delivered powerful keynotes for **corporations, nonprofits, and educational institutions**.

A wife, mother of eleven, and faith-driven leader, Rachel is no stranger to life's twists and turns. In *Back to Me: Evolved & Unshaken – A New Awakening*, she shares her personal journey of resilience, self-discovery, and faith, offering a roadmap for anyone ready to reclaim their story.

Find Rachel online at **racheldfox.com** or connect with her on social media **@racheldfox**.

You can connect with me on:
- https://www.racheldfox.com
- https://www.facebook.com/racheldfox

www.ingramcontent.com/pod-product-compliance
Lightning Source LLC
Chambersburg PA
CBHW020244010526
44107CB00002B/86